THE NEW
ARTICULATE
EXECUTIVE

Look, Act, and Sound
Like a Leader

GRANVILLE N. TOOGOOD

New York   Chicago   San Francisco   Lisbon   London   Madrid   Mexico City
Milan   New Delhi   San Juan   Seoul   Singapore   Sydney   Toronto

The **McGraw·Hill** Companies

For Carolyn and Wayne

3 4 5 6 7 8 9 10 11 12 13 14 15   QFR/QFR   1 9 8 7 6 5 4 3 2 1

ISBN 978-0-07-174326-6
MHID   0-07-174326-X

This publication is designed to provide accurate and authoritative information in regard to the subject matter covered. It is sold with the understanding that neither the author nor the publisher is engaged in rendering legal, accounting, securities trading, or other professional services. If legal advice or other expert assistance is required, the services of a competent professional person should be sought.
—*From a Declaration of Principles Jointly Adopted by a Committee of the American Bar Association and a Committee of Publishers and Associations*

Library of Congress Cataloging-in-Publication Data

Toogood, Granville N.
      The new articulate executive : look, act, and sound like a leader / by Granville Toogood. — 2nd ed.
          p.   cm.
      Includes index.
      ISBN 978-0-07-174326-6
      1. Business communication.   2. Business presentations.   3. Public speaking.   4. Communication in management.   5. Leadership.   I. Title.

      HF5718.T66   2010
      658.4'5—dc22   2010001198

An earlier edition of this book was published under the title *The Articulate Executive*.

Interior design by Monica Baziuk

McGraw-Hill books are available at special quantity discounts to use as premiums and sales promotions or for use in corporate training programs. To contact a representative, please e-mail us at bulksales@mcgraw-hill.com.

This book is printed on acid-free paper.

CONTENTS

PART THREE DELIVERY

PART FOUR AFTER THE SPEECH AND MANAGING THE MEDIA

INTRODUCTION
Where Are We?

NINETEENTH-CENTURY AMERICA WITNESSED the golden age of the orator—peopled by rhetorical giants such as Abraham Lincoln, Mark Twain, Henry Clay, Frederick Douglass, Daniel Webster, John C. Calhoun, and Phillip Brooks, among many others. By the power of their words alone, these masters of the language helped us understand who we are and for generations steered the political and cultural evolution of the great American story.

The twentieth century saw the rapid rise of mass communication and media. Newspaper empires sprang up in the United States and Britain. Science fiction morphed into reality as radio, and then television changed our lives in ways we could never have imagined. A tiny community of orange orchards in California spread the fantastic magic of a new art form called the motion picture around the world.

In the twenty-first century we are still in the pioneering phase of exploring new frontiers as different from radio, TV, and newspapers as talkie color movies were from silent black-and-white films. We are in the dawn of the age of social media. A quick visit to Google will tell you that social media has hundreds of life-forms, endless definitions, thousands of experts, countless books on the subject, and tens of millions, soon perhaps billions, of discrete voices all clamoring to be heard. Social media is a chaotic, jubilant expression of personal freedom and affirmation, a forum for all, a universal ocean of connectivity and interrelationships unlike anything the world has ever seen—and it's getting bigger every day.

Barack Obama was the first U.S. president to successfully surf the wave of social media (until recently also sometimes referred to as new media) and ride it all the way to the White House. As the contest heated up in 2008, his campaign ignited political buzz with chat rooms and posted daily barrages of online clips showing the candidate in action and talking in sound bites. In effect, social media put the candidate "on the air" (in this case, in The Cloud or Ethernet) twenty-four-seven and kept an interactive dialogue of millions of Americans—mostly his target audience of younger voters—stoked and buzzing right up to election day. Some pundits have suggested Obama's success in the voting booth was due in part to his mastery of the new media such as YouTube and Twitter, while the McCain campaign relied far more on "old media," such as newspapers, magazines, and traditional networks.

So social media can be a great political resource, and we will see more of social media in future campaigns. But without a candidate, social media is just a tool and can never take the place of the candidate. Without Obama, social media was just social media.

No one knows how big social media will eventually become, how far it will go, or how it will ultimately effect and influence our behaviors. No doubt social media will present opportunities for future business leaders. But it can never trump flesh-and-blood transactions and interactions. Twitter, Google, Facebook, YouTube, LinkedIn, and more on the way can help market your business—and you—but they can never *be* you.

Social media can *never be*:

> the new CEO who so impresses the analysts that the stock
> soars 20 percent the next day
> the team leader who drives productivity up 15 percent
> the entrepreneur who articulates the vision that shapes a whole
> new industry and makes markets

the salesperson who keeps raising the bar year after year

the coach who breaks through mental barriers to forge a championship team from mediocrity

You may remember the Yankelovich survey that found if you compare two similar companies in the same industry—one with a CEO who is little seen or heard, and the other with a dynamic leader who has the power to command important audiences—the company with the dynamic leader will typically have a market value as much as *double* the market value of the company with the silent, unseen CEO.

No one can achieve this kind of dramatic contrast remotely. Twitter can't do it. Facebook can't do it. LinkedIn can't do it. YouTube can't do it. Even blogs and the Buzz—the word on the Internet "street"—can't do it. Until clones and robots replace us all, only *people* can do this.

Social media is in The Cloud. It is electronic, abstract, and digital and usually revolves around small images you can hold in your hand. It is a good thing and a useful thing, but it is *only a tool.* You, by contrast, are *not* a tool. *You are the authentic article,* large as life, and you must be seen and heard. You may not see yourself as an Abraham Lincoln or Daniel Webster. But you have—as did they—*unlimited potential to lead and go far.* As you will see in these chapters, the wider the spread of social media, the greater your opportunities to position yourself in the world around you, both professionally and personally.

The greatest opportunity of all is to use what you find here to not only position yourself in the twenty-first century, but also to shape it, to become a transformational leader, and ultimately to become what I call a threshold leader. If the transformational leader can enlist others to rally around a cause and accomplish great things, the threshold leader, often alone, is forever out ahead of the fulcrum of change and is in fact the agent of change itself, clearing a path for transformational leaders (enlightened business leaders) to follow.

If you feel yourself drawn to this far frontier—or to wherever your journey may take you—this book should be in your survival pack when you arrive.

EVERYTHING YOU NEED TO KNOW ABOUT PUBLIC SPEAKING

- Seven key errors never to make
- The secret of translation—the real heart of your presentation
- The four As—how to orchestrate your thoughts
- The POWER formula—secrets to the perfect presentation
- Reversing the wave—starting with the end
- Projecting into the future
- How to begin and end
- The "rocket"—how to make your presentation really fly
- The "necklace"—a simple, yet elegant design for any presentation
- The 18-minute wall—and how to get over it
- The 8-second drill—the secret to capturing any audience
- The menagerie of mistakes
- Ten important writing—and speaking—rules to live by
- The most common rhetorical mistakes
- How to beat fear
- Reading a speech without appearing to read
- How to use teleprompters and stage monitors
- Mastering the art of Q&A

PART ONE

THE SPEAKING GAME

1

LEADERSHIP COMMUNICATIONS
The Secret Weapon

LEGENDARY BUSINESS LEADERS share more than just spectacular success. They not only are typically great communicators themselves but recognize and value this precious skill in others.

Former General Electric chairman Jack Welch, often cited as America's most admired CEO—even years after he left the job— once said that the number one quality he looked for in future leaders was, "Someone who is comfortable talking to *anyone*—*anybody* in the world, in New Delhi, Moscow, Cairo, Beijing—*anywhere!*"—in other words, someone who could make things happen across international borders and cultural barriers, someone who could walk into a room anywhere in the world and fix a problem, delight a customer, secure a partner, or close a deal. This, said Welch, is the single most important business asset, absolutely essential to any company that hopes to grow and prosper.

Warren Buffett, the famed Oracle of Omaha and one of the world's wealthiest men, recently told a TV audience of M.B.A. students at his alma mater, the Columbia Business School, that he would offer $100,000 seed money to any student in the audience in return for 10 percent of future earnings. He then upped the ante by declaring that if the recipients could demonstrate what he called "public speaking," or communications skills—or were willing to invest in public speaking training—he would boost his offer to $150,000. Buffett confided to the students that he himself had taken a Dale Carnegie course early in his career and that it was one of the best business investments he had ever made.

Today, Buffett is recognized far beyond the world of business as a brilliant communicator who can explain even the most complex business issues, dense financial engineering, and economic forecasts in terms that even a child can understand. His famous annual newsletter to investors is eagerly anticipated and widely admired for its simplicity, clarity, humor, and wisdom. Investors, business leaders, entrepreneurs, and financial markets the world over hang on his every word and follow his every move. Buffett is the kind of living legend who proves yet again that when you marry brains and talent with outstanding communications skills, the sky's the limit.

That was my message in 1995 with the first edition of *The Articulate Executive,* and it is my message today. But now the message is even more urgent—because technology, for all its glories, is rapidly dumbing us down. It's quietly, insidiously alienating us from one another and robbing us of our precious and unique gifts of face-to-face direct human interaction. We e-mail, Twitter (tweet), fax, text message, play video games, watch TV, and surf YouTube, Facebook, Google, and the Web. These are wondrous miracles of our time, but they come at a price.

The deeper we dive into all the marvelous technology, the farther apart we drift—drawn to the mesmerizing magic of our desktops, laptops, and handhelds—and in a sense the less engaging, singular, unique, and human we become. Our kids text message nonstop—even when they are sitting right next to each other, not even ten inches apart.

Many of us don't read as much, nor socialize the way we used to, nor value speaking skills the way we once did. Even educated Americans—men and women with college and advanced degrees—make grammatical errors in writing and conversation that would not have been tolerated just a generation ago. We forget—and to our peril, hardly value—the simplest and most basic things, such as how to have an intelligent conversation or even how to spell. As just one example, I recently got a brief thank-you note from a thirtyish, Tulane-educated client with twenty-five grammatical and spelling errors. Incredibly, this is not uncommon. But is it acceptable? Should we yield to the tyranny of the universal dumbing down of even our best and brightest?

The gradual loss of the art of conversation we once valued and cherished, and the steady erosion of our capacity to interact effectively at a very personal level, speaks volumes of the age we live in and may eventually change the very nature of civilization as we know it. Of course, it's true that texting with colleagues in the office can be more efficient than running up and down halls to try to make a decision or resolve an issue. It is also true that e-mailing customers on their handhelds can avoid the hassles of telephone tag. But these facilitators and conveniences will never replace the added business value of direct human contact.

The more we rely on technology to do our talking for us, the more we can expect to see the *cost* of that reliance in our business results and performance.

Our computers can help us run our businesses, but they will never get the actual deal done, enlist investors, persuade managements, recruit and retain new customers, nor lead our employees.

In business, management's inability to interact, articulate, persuade, or enlist can have immediate and potentially fatal consequences. The combined effect over time can be an eventual loss of competitiveness and a *negative effect* on the bottom line. At the personal and career levels, smart and talented people lacking these skills will find the odds stacked against them. The disadvantage could be debilitating, even insurmountable.

Excellence in business communications should be as *routine* as excellence in business performance. Many business leaders (like Jack Welch) will tell you that in successful corporations, communication *is* performance. Those who *look*, *act*, and *sound* like leaders will be seen as leaders. And in any career, this is always a very good thing.

If leadership in business is perceived as an asset, then an inability to sell a product or service, command a room, run a meeting effectively, enlist allies, persuade investors, inspire employees, align team members, or compel key audiences gives the perception of no leadership at all. This means that if you have a good idea, you might not be able to sell it. If you have a vision, no one will hear it. If you have a strategy, no one will follow it. So what does it profit us to have what it takes, if no one can take what we have?

Warren Buffett will tell you that when any commodity, such as an asset class or a particular stock, is perceived to be losing value, that's the exact moment smart investors buck the trend and look for value. His purchase of Burlington Northern Santa Fe Railway bucked all the trends. If his long history as a champion investor is any measure, he will probably make yet another killing. Ironically, in business, if almost nowhere else outside politics, leadership communications is another bankable asset that is actually *gaining* in value—precisely because it is becoming such a rare commodity.

Unlike businesspeople, politicians have long understood the value of leadership communications. In fact, word power is their entire stock and trade. If anyone should doubt the power of the word to accomplish great things, witness the incredible phenomenon of Barack Obama, who rose like a rocket from relative obscurity in the middle of a deep recession to become the first African-American president.

Millions of Americans immediately recognized a good thing when they saw it. The majority who voted for him say they did so largely on his extraordinary ability to articulate his vision and reveal his intelligence, clearly define problems and solutions, simplify the complex, rationally debate any issue, engage in intelligent conversation, resonate with the masses, enlist vast support, secure loyal followings, capture the mood of the nation, win over Independents and Republicans alike, enlighten the uninformed, and discuss challenging crises with a cool head. In other words, Obama positioned himself as a capable leader at a critical historical moment when the whole country was crying out for leadership. This is not the kind of thing you can do with just text messages, e-mails, and tweets (although it is true, as we mentioned earlier, that Obama was the first presidential candidate to harness the vast leverage of YouTube and Twitter to reach millions of mostly young voters).

Maybe businesspeople should borrow from the experience of politicians. The question here is, can you walk into a room anywhere, anytime, and make things happen? Wonderful things unfold when people talk face-to-face in private offices, conference rooms, boardrooms, corridors, auditoriums—and yes, even on the golf course. Deals are cut. Decisions are made. Obstacles are cast aside. Whatever the job, the job gets done.

That's why now more than ever is the time to capitalize on the huge added value that leadership communications brings to any business proposition or transaction. As Warren Buffett would certainly concur, it could be the best business investment you ever made. That's what this book is all about.

Read on.

2

BECOMING A PLAYER

I F YOU RUN a business or want to lead any organization and can't play the game, you are competing with a handicap. Not knowing how to play is simply a liability.

Few business leaders play the game better than Steve Jobs, Apple Computer CEO and *Fortune* magazine's CEO of the decade. Steve Jobs can inspire employees, fire up investors, sell his ideas to the media, enlist allies, and forge partnerships behind closed doors. He is so skilled, in fact, that his 2005 commencement address to the graduating class of Stanford University resonated with an entire generation of Americans, and to this day it is remembered as one of the greatest commencement addresses of all time.

It was a lesson in life, a morality tale about discovery, passion, vision, mortality, redemption, and the meaning of existence—all revealed through three simple stories. It wasn't long before almost everybody in that audience began to realize they were sharing in a magical experience the likes of which they had never heard before. At the end, Jobs said simply: "Stay hungry. Stay foolish," and the crowd went wild with a burst of cheering and applause that just wouldn't quit. And in a sense, it never did. Today, the applause rolls on as people the world over continue to talk about Steve Jobs' "famous commencement speech."

One reason the moment was so extraordinary is that it was so unusual: *Jobs is an exception to the rule.* For every Jobs, there are a thousand others who have no idea how to capitalize on their own potentials.

—— SUPERCOMPETENCE ——

Jobs and a few other business superstars have what I call *supercompetence*, which manifests in the three Cs:

1. *Competence.* Are you good at what you do?
2. *Clarity.* Can you see beyond the job? Can you see the road ahead?
3. *Communication.* This is the most critical. Can you connect with important audiences? Can you go the next step and make dreams reality? Can you make things happen?

Competence and clarity by themselves have never led to superstardom in business or even to excellence. For that, you need the third leg of the stool, communication. But it is painfully self-evident that wherever you look today, this vital component is missing. In fact, the communications skills of an alarming number of business leaders is downright lamentable. And that sorry situation permeates right down through the ranks. The problem is so widespread and runs so deep that it can begin even before the bright-eyed graduates Jobs was talking to walk through the doors to their first job interviews.

Supercompetence defines the difference between a good manager and a great leader.

I read somewhere that *more than half* of all job applicants are turned down on the basis of verbal communication skills judged to be less than adequate. If all these people hit a wall (and probably never know the real reason why), it's mind-boggling to imagine how much wasted effort is poured into presentations that fail for the same reason. What if more than half of all the pitches, presentations, speeches, lectures, and assorted other communications all over the world also failed because of poor communications?

What if the number were only half of that? We're still talking about lost productivity and lost opportunity on a staggering scale. Anyone who is serious about his career or his company has got to know how to play the game.

A friend of mine in a midsize company got an assignment to give a new-business presentation but waited until the last minute to prepare the big pitch. He cannibalized other presentations, made hasty notes, threw together a mixed bag of handouts and visual aids, and then rushed to the airport to catch a plane to the prospective client's headquarters in another city. Not surprisingly, the presentation did not go as well as he might have hoped. The order went to a competitor—a loss of more than $65 million in new business.

When I hear stories like that, it seems only fair to ask, what is the nature of true productivity? Is it more productive to apply oneself diligently every day at one's desk with the aggregate long-term rewards of that labor almost impossible to measure? Or is it more productive to set aside more time—perhaps a day or two—to adequately plan, prepare, and practice for a presentation that could be worth more to your company in just one day than all the fruits of an entire lifetime of functional diligence?

Why should we not expect higher quality, speed, and productivity from our communications abilities—just as we routinely expect these things in our businesses? Most of us spend our working lives unaware that we are in fact the message—that how others see us can determine the degree of our success.

The truth is that *three minutes in front of the right audience* can be worth a year at your desk. It's also true that brainpower, talent, and hard work by themselves cannot guarantee success. To do that, you also need to master the speaking game.

So it all comes down to knowledge and choice. It's we ourselves who determine our success in business and in life. It is up to us to understand the value of the speaking game and empower ourselves (because we know no one else will do it for us). Ignore it and watch opportunity slip through our fingers. Or master it and know rewards we may never have dreamed.

If you opt for rewards, prepare to play.

3

FIRST, UNDERSTAND YOUR AUDIENCE

IT USED TO be said of superlawyers Melvin Belli and F. Lee Bailey that they could persuade almost any jury that a guilty person was innocent and an innocent person guilty. Billy Graham took his crusade to the world and claims his ministry has forever changed the lives of millions of people. Now his son Franklin makes the same claim. If you have something to say and say it well, the world will listen.

First, you have to *understand* the people. When you understand the people, you can identify human needs. When you identify human needs, you can appeal to psychology and thus the mind. I'm actually talking here about two minds: *first*, the conscious mind, which happily swims like a fish all day long in a pool of intellectual activity, and *second*, the primal mind, which lurks somewhere in the dark recesses far below the surface. The primal mind hearkens back to hunting, caves, and flickering firelight and perhaps violent death at an early age.

These are two *separate* beings. Guess which one you want to be talking to?

If you guessed the primal mind, you're right, because the primal mind governs our greatest hopes and fears, our loves and hates, our very hearts. The primal mind is like a cagey beast sniffing the wind, trying to pick up the scent of blood. The primal mind is also a mother wolf, gently protecting and suckling her cub with great love. The primal mind reacts to the gut. It *senses* things, vaulting over the oblivious intellectual mind to pick up vital clues and signals. It is driven by our most basic needs: sex, shelter, creativity, power, work, love, hope, food, fear, and fulfillment. It wants to be recognized, to be reassured. It can be lured open like a rose giving itself to the sun or snapped shut like a frightened clam burrowing itself deeper into the mud.

Go for the heart, and the mind will follow.

This is the fellow we are dealing with. This fellow doesn't listen to our data, to our arguments, to our appeals. He's not interested in our intellectual aplomb. He doesn't really care if we're smart or even if we're dumb. Yet this is the guy, whether we know it or not—or whether we like it or not—who actually makes most of our important decisions for us—and the conscious mind be damned.

This is the guy who acts on *warm feelings* and on *deep dislike*. He's the profoundly unknowable Instinct Man (or Woman) inside each of us. He's the one who kicks the tire and decides to buy the new car; the one who steps through the door, says, "This is it!" and decides to buy the new house; the one who shakes the hand and knows right then and there that this is the right person for the new job. In other words, this is the guy who makes all the important decisions and runs our lives. Once he's made up his mind, there's no going back. He simply says, "This is my decision," retreats back into the murky depths, and alerts the intellectual mind to make a list of ways to justify that decision.

That's why this is the guy we really want to be talking to. And there are only two ways we can get through to him as he sits out there in the audience:

1. Through ourselves (Does he like me?)
2. Through direct appeal to the emotions (stories and anecdotes that touch his heart and poke him in the gut)

——— TALKING TO INSTINCT MAN ———

The good speaker is always on the alert for opportunities to appeal to common sense and our deepest needs. Advertising people understand this principle better than most:

> They're not selling soap. They're selling sex.
> They're not selling perfume. They're selling love.
> They're not selling cars. They're selling excitement.
> They're not selling jeans. They're selling adventure.
> They're not selling cigarettes. They're selling freedom.

And a corporate person isn't selling just strategic plans or making budget proposals or giving quarterly reports. The corporate person is selling confidence, a sense of well-being, of goodwill. In other words, the corporate person is forever selling *himself* or *herself.* To enlist the support of listeners, the corporate person has to try to know the listeners' most basic needs.

Every member of every audience will silently ask the question, "What's in it for me?" Profit sharing? Safety? Wisdom? A chance for promotion? A way to be recognized? To get rich? To find satisfaction? To grow intellectually or spiritually? Try to answer that question. Then shape the path to your own objectives around the Instinct Man. History is full of people who have done exactly that.

THE IMPORTANCE OF BEING HONEST

If Instinct Man is the gatekeeper—and we know he is always hovering out there somewhere with his finger perpetually poised over the "Reject" button—then how do we get him to like us?

If you are worried you may have no charisma, don't give it a second thought. Charisma is *not* the issue; in business, *likability* is the issue. Likability does not depend on charisma. In fact, there is often no correlation between the two. What I call business likability is the critical screening or checkpoint we all have to pass before people will actually buy our ideas. Likability begins with honesty.

So trying to relax and be genuine and truthful with your audience is a good place to start. People expect us to be no different on stage or at the conference table than when we are chatting with them backstage or in the corridors at work. Steve Jobs understands this.

Ask yourself, what is it about you that people seem to respond to? Your straightforwardness? Your humor? Your candor? Your thoughtfulness? Your gentle nature? Your insight? Your passion? These are all real and bankable assets. Whatever assets you bring to the table, be sure to exploit them. In the end, it all comes down to *just being yourself.*

The best way to be yourself is engage in what I call barroom talk. I'm not suggesting you behave like a boozer. I'm just suggesting you imagine yourself in a comfortable situation with friends over a beer in a bar, and imagine trying to enlist them to see things your way on a particular issue or idea. If you feel passion, show it. If you don't, don't try to act as if you do.

Before people will buy your service or your product, they've got to first buy you.

If you can forget about how you are doing and think only of what you are *saying*, you need never feel like you have to act out some imagined role in front of any audience. Have faith in your *message*. Have faith in your *knowledge*. Have faith in yourself.

Everybody today—and I mean everybody—craves authenticity. In the smarmy wake of financial-services scam king Bernie Madoff, and after years of hedge fund scandals, absence of ethics, chronic impropriety, and general misbehavior on Wall Street and in corporate life everywhere, candor, openness, and honesty are at a premium like never before. Steve Jobs understands this, too. He understood this long before Madoff did and all the way back when he first emerged with a computer and a vision from his parents' garage in California.

If there are occasions when you cannot, or will not, be honest with your audience, Instinct Man will probably find you out. In the course of your professional life, you may well discover yourself in this kind of compromising situation. But don't worry. All is not lost—as we will see in later chapters.

It is important to never forget that you are *not making a presentation*. Presentations do not bring us together. They only drive us farther apart. (You will hear me refer to presentations countless times in this book because I must use that word for clarity. But when you read "presentation," you can think "*conversation.*") Nobody wants to hear a presentation, but we all welcome a good conversation—even though you may be the one doing most of the talking.

Steve Jobs does not make presentations, even when he is presenting. He is always having a conversation, and he's always got something to say. He talks without guile. He comes across as a natural. That's why people listen and remember. With important audiences like investors, customers, employees, and the trade press, this is an enormous business asset.

Presentations and conversations are very different animals—as different as the ugly duckling and the pretty swan in the fairy tale. The trick is to create a swan from an ugly duck. So you want to abandon the flawed notion that presentations are desirable—and then put the idea of presentations out of your mind altogether (you will find out how shortly).

Great presentations, masked as conversations, always get you closer to your audience. The closer you get, the better the chance you get what you want.

The more natural and true to yourself you are, the more likely even skeptical audiences will warm to you. Instinct Man, always vigilant, will probably accept you if just do him the simple kindness of not coming across as totally unprepared, scared to death, or a complete phony.

Steve Jobs is always prepared, comfortable with himself and his message, and seen as the genuine article every time. **Moral:** *the real deal is more likely to land the deal.*

—— THE END RUN ——

Next, how do we do an end run around the head and go straight to the heart? *By appealing directly to whatever issue is presenting itself.* What is the issue? What is the source of pain, frustration, anger, dissatisfaction? Do you see a problem? Do you see a solution? What is the need? Identify the need, and you can take a position. Take a position, and you can provide an answer. Provide an answer, and you can enlist support. Enlist support, and you lead.

If you are a great leader, sometimes you lead people *to think for themselves.* For example, say you run a blanket factory for a big textile company. Your entire industry is struggling, the company itself is not doing very well, and you know the factory is failing in spite of everything you've been doing to try and stop the slide. What do you do?

That's exactly the difficult position in which Bob Dale, who later became president of Fieldcrest, found himself. Long before empowerment became a popular management strategy, Bob followed his gut instincts: he took his case to the workers on the factory floor and let them help figure it out.

He said something like: "We've got problems. We're all in this together. You guys know these machines. You're all good at what you do. I want you to put your heads together and let your brains and your magic and your creativity help get us out of this mess."

The workers had never heard a boss talk to them like that. They went right to work with inspired gusto and shortly came up with a brand-new blanket much thicker and softer than anything else on the market at the time. Even the weave and the textiles were new. The new product sold like hotcakes, and the plant and jobs were saved.

But not every story is so upbeat. In the hard world we live in, sometimes we've got to justify pain to the ones who feel it the most.

If you are a boss in a time of downsizing, for instance, you must dampen the flames of fear by talking about job security, consolidation, corporate stability, future opportunity, teamwork, and shared goals to those lucky ones who escape the ax. To those who must go, there's the message of referrals, outplacement services, retirement options, and severance packages, and a candid explanation of why this terrible thing had to happen. If your audience sees you as part of the problem, at least they might also see you as a stand-up person with a heart who wasn't afraid to tell the truth to their faces.

One of my clients found himself throwing his prepared remarks away after his company had taken over another company in a hostile leveraged buyout. Thousands of people had been let go. The audience was a combination of clashing cultures. The mood was uneasy.

He was supposed to talk about the company's financial health, PowerPoint and all. But instead he told a story about how his little boy had found him unable to sleep, sitting downstairs in the dark, worrying about having to fire so many people from both companies in the weeks ahead. It was the first time his son had ever seen him so vulnerable, he said. The son, confused and worried, put his arm over his father's shoulder and said, "It's all right, Dad. It's got to be all right—because I know if it wasn't, you wouldn't do it."

Then the boy told his father why he, too, had been unable to sleep. Just that very day his best friend in fifth grade had been killed after falling out of a third-floor window. The boy talked quietly about his friend and his sense of shock and loss, not yet fully able to comprehend that his friend was gone forever. The father listened. In the end, the boy said, "He never had a life—at least the people in your company have a life. . . ."

"At that moment," the father told his audience, "I knew I had a message. I didn't feel good about what had to be done, but I was able—at least, emotionally—to put it into proper perspective.

"The message is that we all have a future, those who are with us today—and those who are not. For those of us who stay, the future has never been brighter. For those who have left us, we hope we have been a stepping-stone on their journeys to even greater opportunity."

And so it went. The story touched everybody in the audience for several reasons: It reached down into their emotions to wake up the Instinct Man, gave them all a sense of solidarity and a kind of kinship, and served as a life experience that they could all identify with and share together. Most important, it said the man doing the talking was a real human being, and it helped defuse some of the lingering anxieties in the wake of the leveraged buyout.

4

ALPHA DOGS AND WORKER BEES

F ROM THE TIME he was seven, Alex had a dream. He wanted to run his own video game company—and before he was twenty, he did. After only one year in college, Alex dropped out, partnered with a classmate, got seed money from family and friends, and created a video game company that created a niche market. For Alex, work was fun, and fun was work. At twenty-four, after years of eighteen-hour workdays and no time off, he sold the company for $168 million. Thanks to his tireless vision and passion, Alex had no trouble enlisting support and a following. Two years later, even in the face of a daunting recession, he was already building a second successful venture, this time creating a new platform for social media.

Sam worked for Alex. Age thirty-eight and unmarried, he had an M.B.A. and Ph.D. in environmental sciences. Sam was the assistant controller. He enjoyed his work but liked to spend all his downtime backpacking, rock climbing, kayaking, and skiing. For Sam, work paid the bills and made possible the things he really cared about. He had no desire to run anything or lead anyone. His priorities were clear, and he was happy. When Alex sold the company, Sam moved on to another company and a similar job. He's still happy.

Not everyone is born to be a leader like Alex, *but almost everyone can learn how.* If you choose to lead, then you can move to the head of the line—simply by practicing protocols that can help take you there.

You are the change agent and the visionary, the one who will create new industries, help people navigate through tough times, and pave the way for ongoing growth and a successful future. You are the potential alpha dog. You may even be the transformative leader or possibly even the threshold leader.

On the other hand, if like Sam you elect not to be a leader, for any number of reasons, then good for you. Without you, business would grind to a halt and the entire country would shut down. You are the worker bee, content in your role as functionary, collecting the paycheck, and enjoying your time off.

But for the potential alpha dogs—for those willing to accept the challenge, risk, and reward of thinking large and reaching high—you still need to understand what it takes to position yourself as a leader. As I have said, *brains and talent alone will not necessarily cut it.*

If I had to give America's future business leaders the best advice in the shortest time, this is what I would tell them:

1. *Understand who you really are and what you really want.* Are you an alpha dog or worker bee? Choose one and be happy with your choice (if you are reading this, you are likely a potential alpha dog).
2. *Do you have a vision?* Leaders need a vision. They need to see, as Bill Gates says, the road ahead. Then they need to know how to get down the road. To do that, they need to know how to articulate a road map for that vision that others will follow. If they can't articulate, they can't lead.

3. *Do you have the chops to play in the same arena with other potential alpha dogs?* Do you have the kind of commitment it takes to play for higher stakes and go the distance?

If you can pass this little quiz, then you are a player. But to be a winner, you have to master certain truths.

First, I would tell you: *worker bees deal in information; leaders deal in knowledge.* For example, the floor worker will tell you how many units she assembles on a given day. The team or division leader will gather that information to create a knowledge bucket that explores possible new game changers, such as improved manufacturing techniques, product development, and potential new markets.

Leaders understand that the gap between idea and action is huge. President John Kennedy used to complain that even as president he had a tough time making things happen—and this is coming from one of our most articulate presidents ever. So leaders know they can't sit still. If they expect action, they know they have to bridge the gap.

Leaders know that they are always selling not only their ideas, but also their organizations and themselves. Great leaders create a party line around themselves, a marquis message that everybody can rally behind. Some, like Steve Jobs of Apple, Bill Gates of Microsoft, and Warren Buffett of Berkshire Hathaway, get so good at all three that they actually become the company and a brand name themselves. In the end, they become the vision itself.

I would also tell you that if you plan to lead people in a common corporate or political cause, *you first have to own the hearts.* Get the hearts, and the minds follow.

To do that, the best leaders share critical best leadership communications practices. Among other things they:

- Know that to get things done, they have to command any stage or conference room, and persuade any audience to enlist wide collaboration and support.
- Understand and identify with the needs of their employees, customers, managements, partners, and investors. In other words, like President Obama, they speak in the language of *we*.
- Recognize that the answer to transformation and success depends not just on technology or even innovation, but ultimately in themselves.
- Seek every opportunity to get out of the office and down on the floor, or up on the stage, or into the interview, or on the industry conference panel to enlist as many confederates as possible. The wider the net, the greater the influence, and the greater the opportunity.

Now let's see how we can put these principles into play.

5

AVOIDING
DANGEROUS TRAPS

A FEW YEARS AGO a vice president of a Fortune 10 company spent a solid month preparing for his first big presentation to the chairman. For thirty days he focused his concentration and productivity time into building something he wasn't quite sure how to build.

When the big day finally came, it was the second day of a long, two-day marathon of presentations. The time was 4:50 Friday afternoon. The vice president was so consumed with the moment and the fast-approaching culmination of all his recent efforts that he failed to correctly gauge the mood in the room. He did not notice, for example, that some of the senior officers were stirring restlessly and impatiently glancing at their watches. Even after a forgettable start to his forty-minute-plus presentation and the chairman's curt interruption to request that he speed things up and get to the point (because some people had to catch planes), the vice president marched doggedly onward. Apparently fired by fear of failure and too rigorously prepared to be flexible, he seemed not to have heard the chairman's admonition.

Meanwhile, waves of thinly disguised impatience swept the room. Soon it became apparent even to the hapless vice president that things were threatening to slip out of control. After ten minutes, when the vice president had apparently still not gotten to the point, the chairman rang down the curtain. He put an end to the meeting, an end to the presentation, and as it turned out, an end to the vice president's career in the company.

——— SEVEN KILLER NO-NOS ———

The lesson here was a need for flexibility and perhaps even an entirely new approach in a world where change is a daily fact of life and every second counts. Several elements conspired to make things go badly for the vice president:

1. *His presentation was designed improperly.* He never would have had the problems he did had he simply reversed the order—in other words, he should have begun with the conclusion. That, after all, is what his audience was waiting to hear—but never did.
2. *He had planned to speak too long—forty minutes.* A maximum of eighteen minutes, plus twenty-two minutes of question and answer (Q&A), would have served him better.
3. *He used too many visual aids.* Not only that, but he used them incorrectly and picked the wrong ones.
4. *He tried to talk about too much.*
5. *He allowed the presentation itself to dominate everything—even himself.* He forgot about the big picture, the message, and the main points, instead focusing only on the mechanics of trying to tell too much detail—an exercise I liken to trying to force an elephant into a golf bag. The presentation overwhelmed him and subsequently overwhelmed his audience.
6. *On top of all that, he had no theme, no "takeaway" that could be remembered a week later.*

7. *As if that weren't enough—for all his preparation, his basic lack of faith in his own presentation showed, and he came across as uncomfortable and nervous.*

So despite all his best efforts, he failed. Instead of seizing an opportunity, he walked into a series of common traps and wound up a victim of his own undoing. Just a few simple guidelines, covered in this book, might well have saved the day.

PART TWO

CREATING THE PERFECT PRESENTATION

6

GET IT TOGETHER

I ONCE GOT A call from an $11 billion operating arm of a big manu-
facturing company. They explained that their main competition,
a large producer of aircraft engines, was eating their business for
breakfast, lunch, and dinner. The market share was roughly 85/15.
Something was clearly amiss. Could it be that their new business
and client presentations needed work? Would I come and take a
look?

I flew out to the client, sat in on a couple of key presentations,
and wound up stunned by an apparent paradox: how could such
intelligent, competent men and women—top managers, division
heads, talented engineers—be so patently inept? I came up with a
long laundry list of things I thought might help turn the situation
around, got the OK to proceed, and went to work.

For the next several months I met with groups of managers (no
more than six at a time to ensure quality) for a total of three days for
each group. I let them witness their own presentations on video playback and then led them through a series of steps to change their
thinking, their focus, their procedures, their planning process, their
attitudes and objectives, and other categories that needed fixing. We
developed a consistent business message, threw out most of the slides,
shortened the presentations, practiced basic talking skills, redesigned
the few remaining visuals, began using anecdotal evidence, intro-

duced a conversational style, got to the point fast, ended strongly, and more. Then top management sent them all back out into the field.

Eighteen months later, the market share was almost exactly reversed. I do not claim credit for that reversal—though I would like to. The company made a good product. They were able to keep quality while cutting costs, and management made the right moves at the right times. But it did not hurt that roughly three dozen senior engineers who spearheaded the sales and customer service teams were now a lot smarter and a lot more effective in how they presented themselves, their products and services, their company, their profession, and even their industry.

I believe our success in that instance was due, in part, to the fact that we tried to make the presentations easy to understand and remember. Our aim, as always, was *simplicity*, *economy*, *impact*, and *focus*.

—— CAN YOU TRANSLATE? ——

Regardless of whether your presentation is elegant and streamlined or fat and burdened with unnecessary numbers and statistics, your first responsibility to your audience is to serve as a *translator*. This is the *added value* that any good presenter brings to the party. Translation is also the engine that propels the rocket (which we will talk more about later) and then drives it all the way to its target.

The translator *demystifies* the esoteric to the lay audience. For example, a speaker explaining the complexities of a merger and acquisitions deal to an audience of, say, civil engineers, would do well to couch everything in simple concepts and plain language. The translator should carefully highlight every step, explain why, assume nothing, and monitor progress by constantly asking the question, "Would I be getting this if I were there listening to me?"

Or rather than make a conventional presentation to senior management, an assistant vice president might choose to go the next logical step and take a particular point of view. This would boost the value of the presentation—because rather than simply present-ing facts and data, now she is making specific strategic recommen-dations based on that data. This tactic by itself would not only be helpful to management, but also cast the presenter as a potential future leader.

—— THE SNOW JOB ——

An executive friend of mine complained recently that a manage-ment consultant he was considering hiring gave a presentation that seemed not only inane, but pointless. My friend felt suffocated—buried under an avalanche of statistical information presented in a PowerPoint extravaganza packed with endless rows of hard-to-read numbers. For three hours he suffered under this onslaught; then he confided later that he felt pretty stupid because he was unable to figure out what the guy was trying to say.

I assured my friend that the problem lay not with him but with the consultant (who, as you might imagine, did not get the job). Either out of ignorance or sheer devious intent, the consultant had "snowed" my friend with enough random facts to ruin a good half-day's productivity, perhaps hoping that the appearance of arcane knowledge would substitute for a lack of competence.

Had he been a good translator and explained in eighteen min-utes or less (see Chapter 14, "The 18-Minute Wall") how the num-bers told a story that could help his would-be client, my guess is that the consultant would have had the job. *So translate and prosper—and watch your clients prosper.*

—— DUMP THE DATA DUMP ——

The fact is that most people are turned off by endless rafts of infor-mation, as we witnessed in the consultant story. Data dumps are generally held to be arrogant and selfish, because they make the audience do all the work. Most audiences rightfully resent having to unravel and piece together whatever you are trying to tell them. Data dumps typically tell us way more than we will ever have to know. It's kind of like using a shotgun to hit the barn—hoping some of the pellets somehow find their marks.

By contrast, people appreciate it when you take the time to understand their wants, speak directly to their needs, and dump the data dump. Suddenly, the data dump might magically morph into just a handful of numbers and a couple of graphs, and a simple message. *All you need is to understand the need.*

For example, in my own area of expertise I might try to recognize a need by asking the question: What does it profit us if employees, customers, and shareholders don't hear what we're trying to tell them? A manager might ask: Why are we failing? What do we have to do to turn the situation around? What is the solution? A salesperson might ask customers: What can we do to serve you better? How can we improve our processes, services, and responsiveness? Are we exceeding your expectations?

Once you think you know the need, you may have your message. Once you have your message, you can stand for something. Once you stand for something, you have set yourself apart from the average speaker—even if you may think you are not a particularly good speaker yourself.

For instance, David Kearns, the former CEO of Xerox, saw a need for better education. Virtually every business speech he gave focused on that simple theme. He came to be known as the "education CEO." He stood for something, and no matter what he was talking about, his topic was just another way of saying that we have to beef up our K-12 education process in this country—for the sake of business, for the country, and for the world.

Barack Obama identified a deep national need for new leadership and positioned himself successfully to meet that need. With unusually compelling rhetorical skills—even for a politician—he portrayed himself as a maverick thinker, made an asset of his inexperience in Washington, and convinced millions of undecided voters he alone could lead the country through a host of national crises, from two unresolved wars to an economy teetering on the brink.

Bill Clinton's entire first campaign came down to just one sentence, "It's the Economy, Stupid" (a takeoff on the old acronym *KISS*, "Keep It Simple, Stupid"). Clinton's job was not easy. First he had to explain to the American people exactly what the problem was, how it got that way, why it had to be fixed, and then how it had to be fixed. With every audience he identified the need and then logically presented his case. By contrast, his opponent, George H. Bush, was unable to talk about the economy in the same way, because publicly he took the position that the problem didn't exist. Or if it did exist, it would just fix itself.

People will sit still for almost anything—even increased taxes—
if you are able to explain satisfactorily the need and
logic behind your actions.

So in your own presentations, even if you're giving only a routine quarterly status report, try to stand for something. Try to spot a need; then explain how to satisfy that need. In a business talk, look for changes, trends, or developments. Do these changes present an emerging need? What is the best way to answer these needs and appeal to the audience?

Why are sales off, for example? Could it be the economy—or do we have a problem in productivity, manufacturing, research and development, quality control, distribution, or all of the above? Your need is whatever it takes to beat the problem. You take a position when you use the persuasive power of logic to help people see the problem the way you do and then take action to fix it.

You're already beginning to sound like a leader.

IMPORTANT QUESTIONS
—— THAT DETERMINE ——
EFFECTIVENESS

So to be a player, you need to evaluate, interpret, translate, and project (more on projection later).

A good translator is like a good surgeon—excising unwelcome elements with a steady hand and executing every move with precision and economy.

Translation enables the metamorphosis from information to knowledge. To translate effectively, you have to ask questions:

- What does this really mean?
- Why is this important?
- What should I really be saying here?
- What is the point?
- Does this add anything?
- Am I speaking in a language everyone can understand?
- Am I using examples that fit?
- Who really cares?

If you can't answer these questions, you are doing yourself and your audience a disservice.

Even worse, if you can't answer these questions, you might resort to the unthinkable and unload a data dump. Shame on you if you do.

—— THE FOUR As ——

Ask the right questions and the truth will come out. You may be able to see situations and trends you didn't see before. You will force yourself to be crisp, to find the path of least resistance. Every piece of information will tell a small story that is part of a bigger story. It is up to you to orchestrate the essential details, head them all in the same direction, and walk them carefully where they've got to go. Think of it this way:

- ◆ **Assemble**—Bring the relevant data together.
- ◆ **Align**—Make certain all the facts are headed in the same direction.
- ◆ **Apply**—Explain how these facts, put together, tell a story.
- ◆ **Assign**—Go the next step and add value. That is, take the information and what it is telling you; then project that information into a highly probable future reality. You add value to the entire proposition by creating a model for the future that will let us make decisions today.

Put it all together, and you are ready to start unleashing the power.

7

DESIGNING
THE PERFECT
PRESENTATION
The POWER Formula

THE MOST NEGLECTED portion of any presentation is typically the preparation, for two reasons: (1) preparation takes time—and busy people often prefer to risk "winging it" than to spend time on something that may not reward them, and (2) they don't have the slightest idea how to put the thing together in the first place—other than by resorting to some bad habits that, like a bad cold, they may have picked up along the way. So preparation can be boring and is not always seen to be productive.

But if someone were to offer those busy people a quick, easy way to assemble their thoughts intelligently and allow them to be consistently effective, they would likely invest a little more effort to realize a big payback. Wouldn't it be nice, for example, if you could follow the same basic blueprint every time and know that your presentations would be half as long but three times as effective? Wouldn't it also be nice to know that you would never again have to spend two weeks or a month agonizing over the preparation of a big presentation or speech?

Come to think of it, wouldn't it be nice if we could be certain that every audience got our message right the first time, every time, and that they could pass a quiz on what you said when they left the room? Maybe even remember a month or six months later what the message was?

You can enjoy these big paybacks simply by designing your presentation with five key elements in mind:

1. Strong start
2. One theme
3. Good examples
4. Conversational language
5. Strong ending

These are the key building blocks that constitute the perfect presentation. The perfect presentation is a reality within the reach of anyone willing to stretch.

Think of these five elements as an acorn. Plant that acorn in your head, and watch the acorn grow into an oak tree. That oak tree is a fail-safe technology for busy executives I call the *POWER formula*. Put another way, the POWER formula is like a tool kit for your brain. It can fix what doesn't work—and fine-tune what does—and should be with you whenever you have the opportunity to speak.

8

THE STRONG START

Wᴴᴇɴ ʏᴏᴜ ʙᴇɢɪɴ your presentation or speech, you don't have to be funny and you don't have to be clever. But you should never, ever be *boring*. So to make sure you don't get off on the wrong foot with your audience, plunge right in.

The POWER formula goes like this:

—— *P* STANDS FOR PUNCH ——

To galvanize the minds of the audience, you've got to strike quickly. We have already talked briefly about the philosophical need for a strong start. Here are eight specific ways to begin with a punch:

1. Begin with the ending. In other words, the *conclusion* goes first. Start with a strong statement that embraces your message. Omega becomes alpha, alpha-omega—the start and finish become one.

This is perhaps the strongest way to begin business presentations, which are typically rated for their clarity and straightforwardness. Nothing could be clearer than an uncompromising statement that says it all. Nothing could be more straightforward than cutting straight to the core within just a matter of seconds. And nothing could make your job of transferring some kind of news to your audience easier than a summary statement that presents the conclusion first.

Getting to the point seems to be a big obstacle in too many presentations. Failing to get quickly to the point does not appeal to the busy people listening, nor does it bode well for the presenter or for the presentation itself. All too often we find that a presentation that early on seems to lack a clear theme actually has no theme at all upon closer examination.

In these poorly designed presentations, a sense of gathering frustration begins to build in the audience. Frustration leads to irritation, and if things don't improve, the audience is left feeling cheated. Think of the hours, weeks, months, even sometimes years of our lives we have given to ineffectual meetings and presentations that we later could remember only as "a waste of time."

You need never waste people's time again if you make it your business to tell them quickly everything they have to know. For example, let's say you're a sales team leader about to make a monthly sales report to your senior management.

DON'T BEGIN WITH: *"It's nice to be here today. In my remarks I would like to discuss the sales outlook and . . ."*

RATHER, HOW ABOUT STARTING WITH: *"China and India are the keys to our future. Next year we expect the China market to open up completely and India two years after that. Right now we have only a 2 percent penetration in China and roughly one-half of 1 percent in India, so there's a lot of room for growth. In fact, we expect to capture 30 percent of the market in both countries within five years."*

That's the bottom line. You just made the bottom line your top line (headline?) and your conclusion your beginning.

Is your company at a crossroads?

INSTEAD OF: *"Today I would like to talk about implementing our strategic plan and review the committee recommendations,*

then discuss our contractual obligations with our union, and . . ."
(Yawn.)

WHY NOT SAY: *"Our choice is clear. Either we make big changes*
starting today and dominate the industry once again—or we
keep on doing what we're doing and run the risk of going out of
business in two years."

Too strong? Inappropriate? Maybe—depending on the circumstances. But in my view it is a far, far better thing to get right to the point and run the risk of being identified as a high-potential individual than stay forever a slave to convention and a source of boredom to busy people.

If you are reporting up within your organization and your presentations are viewed as anything other than good, you are doing a disservice to the senior people you are reporting to. You are probably also doing yourself a disservice, which could eventually be reflected in your job status or compensation. If you are reporting down, a mushy message could be seen as an inability to lead. So to avoid any chance of being accused of obfuscation, begin with a real bang.

The chair of one of the giant companies I work with has the reputation of being extremely impatient, especially when he sets time aside to hear business reviews and presentations. His senior officers have learned through bitter experience to get right to the point.

The rule is, tell the big picture in the first forty-five seconds; then spend the rest of the time explaining how you came to that conclusion—what I call "reversing the wave" (more on that later).

In one particular case, a corporate vice president who ran a $3 billion operating company was scheduled to make his first quarterly review. He spent days agonizing over the piles of data, preparing an elaborate PowerPoint show, working and reworking his material, adding and subtracting information, changing the text, editing, and generally driving himself crazy.

But when the big day came, his message was garbled in a mountain of data, and he seemed to take forever to get to his point. Afterward the audience spent more time talking about how tedious his presentation was rather than about what he actually said. Another key opportunity lost and another presentation that certainly did more harm than good.

2. Tell a personal story that makes a business point. This does not mean trying to be funny. Telling your own story is certainly one of the *most* engaging and personal ways to capture the attention of any audience. Say, for example, that you want to make the point that globalization is an essential ingredient for the future success of your company. You might begin (after a pause) this way:

> *When I was shopping at Harrods in London on a recent business trip, I noticed that even though the shelves were filled with merchandise, I wasn't able to find any of our own products—no matter how hard I tried.*
>
> *By contrast, yesterday I was in Bloomingdale's in New York, and our products filled the display cases of the cosmetics section.*
>
> *The problem is that in London, people were buying. In New York, Bloomingdale's was practically empty, and the cash registers were silent.*
>
> *You don't have to be a business school graduate to see that there's a basic economic sea change in progress here.*

In this case you are sounding a kind of wake-up call to your audience, drawing their attention to the need for global strategic planning within your organization or perhaps within your industry.

This is the kind of beginning that might work, let's say, for a marketing vice president speaking to a trade association.

3. Use an anecdote, illustration, or analogy—not a personal story—to make your business point. This might include something you read in the paper, heard on the radio, or saw on TV or something somebody told you. For example, to make your point about the need to go global you might say:

> *I read in the paper yesterday that one of every three U.S. companies now gets half its revenues from operations overseas—and that overseas trend is only expected to continue.*
>
> *But if you look at our industry, the reverse seems to be true—and that reverse trend can spell trouble for each of us here today.*

Again, you are making a case—this time by drawing on the world of information around you to drive home a point.

4. Use a quotation to start. We are not talking here about Aristophanes or Tennyson. Quoting famous people can be seen as cutesy and manipulative. But on occasion, you might be able to get away with something like:

> *Thomas Jefferson once said that the great joy of being an American was simply having freedom of choice. . . . Well, I am sure that if Jefferson were alive today, he would certainly agree that at no other time in our history have we had more chance to choose our future opportunities than right now.*
>
> *I am talking about the abundance of opportunities that await us—if we recognize that the future success of our business depends almost exclusively upon how well we sell our products overseas.*

But you are better off looking for something more newsworthy, current, and strictly business. Find a quote from an industry leader, media source, trade paper, or government official. For example:

> *You may have noticed yesterday in the* Financial Times *that Fed Chairman Bernanke said our future as the world's greatest*

economy and most powerful nation will be determined by just two things: our ability to discipline our markets and ourselves.

If Chairman Bernanke is correct, our industry had better get started right now because we've got a lot of work to do.

5. Use a rhetorical question. This old device works every time. The question is intended to jolt the audience to pay attention right away.

A rhetorical question is a question simply for its own sake. It is what it says—a rhetorical device that need not have a real answer. Its sole reason for existence is to *highlight* an issue. For example:

Why is it that every time I meet businesspeople from Asia or Europe, they keep asking me why America has decided to stay out of global markets?

Well, the answer is that America is very much in global markets. The problem is that while we may believe it, it seems that almost no one else in the world does. . . . And why is that? (Pause) Because we still can't compete.

So the speaker is quickly setting up a proposition: We think we are global, but the rest of the world does not. We think we can compete in the international marketplace, but the rest of the world apparently does not. The rest of the speech, if played properly, will dance to one song: here is the problem as I see it, and here is what I think we ought to do about it.

6. Project into the future. The world loves a seer, and audiences are no different. Take a flyer and try to make a prudent estimate of things to come: do you see changes, new situations, different conditions ahead? The most prudent among us might venture to cast their auguring nets only several years out, in the event their projections are dead wrong. But some of today's most successful business speakers and authors position themselves as flat-out futurists. They have no problem looking out 50, even 150, or 200 years into the future, where you can be sure they are safe. Surely if you predict events just twenty years down the road, you may be fairly secure in the knowledge that the majority of your listeners won't remember—or care— what you said way back when. (Besides, they might not even be around to have an opinion.)

So go ahead and have a little fun—with the right audience. People love to believe they have had a glimpse into the future, and if you follow your strong lead with credible evidence based on sensible presumptions and current facts, you might even be able to convince yourself that what you see coming will really happen. For example:

> *Thirty years from now, the company you work for probably will not exist. Your workweek will be just three days. You will work at a computer terminal in your home office two of those days, with the third day devoted to meetings with fellow work associates via videoconferencing and in production centers run by corporate city-states. You will spend another two days energizing and brainstorming in think tanks run like round-the-clock conference centers by corporate city-states.*

That's quite a picture you've just painted. Arguable, but interesting enough to make me want to hear more. For all you know it might actually come true—because some of these seemingly wild premises may have some foundation in fact, based on what we are already beginning to see.

Going back for a moment to our centerpiece of globalization, it would not be difficult to provide an intelligent link between our dramatic future depiction and how these great changes could be the eventual result of worldwide political, economic, social, and spiritual shifts we can feel even now.

You should note, by the way, that people who like to position themselves as leaders, whether in business or politics, are also *fond of future projection* and don't hesitate to jump right in where others may fear to tread. So feel free. Jump right in with them.

7. Look into the past. Looking into the past is another way people who see themselves as leaders attempt to justify their stewardship. But I am not talking about looking into the past in the conventional sense. The key here is to define the past to *reveal change.*

Leaders understand change. One reason they are leaders is that they make it their business to identify changes in progress.

If you can do that consistently, the world needs you—because people like you can harness history, control it just enough not to get run over by it. With luck, people like you can put inevitable change and evolution to good use.

A good leader's self-image is as someone who has the big picture, a historical perspective—someone who can command a worldview, size things up before they become a problem, take action in advance of need (what some businesspeople call "being proactive"). Corporate CEOs love to see themselves as statesmen, powers not only in their own corporate backyards, but real players on the world stage. I have written many a speech for many a corporate chief that sweeps through fifty or sixty years in just a few seconds—giving the unmistakable message to audiences that here is a person who has his act together. For example:

> *In 1970, the Japanese had just 2 percent of the worldwide telecommunications business. But by 1995, Koreans and Japanese commanded 42 percent of the telecommunications business around the world.*
>
> *If this trend continues, we can expect that by the year 2015 the Koreans will dominate—and we might not even be in the telecommunications business.*
>
> *That to me is a bad dream that doesn't have to come true. And that's why I'm here today—to send a wake-up call to every sena-*

tor and representative in Washington. To compete globally we have got to have a level playing field. Right now. Today.

Bingo. Point made, forge ahead, drive hard to the finish, and then finish hard.

8. Humor. Humor is *very high risk, and I don't recommend it.* Even the funniest, most facile speakers sometimes wind up sounding sarcastic, insensitive, snide, or downright dumb when they try to get a laugh. If a joke goes wrong, for any number of different reasons, the unfortunate result is often a weak, pathetic kind of embarrassed tittering that is mostly an awkward expression of sympathy for the hapless speaker. When an early joke goes flat, it tends to take all the bubbles out of whatever follows.

Why do so many people insist on starting a speech with a joke? One, they see others do it, so they think it is the way to go. Two, they simply don't know of any other way to start strongly. And three, they think a joke will "break the ice" (it can, but probably not in the way they intended).

Even when a speaker is smart enough to use humor to make a legitimate business point, there are other mines in the minefield. Suggestive humor is out of bounds, but it never ceases to amaze me how many people still don't get it.

For example, I heard a speaker tell a joke about a woman sunbathing naked on a skylight to make the point that there are two sides to every issue. Nice try. But I could hardly believe my ears. Technically, his execution was correct. The story made a point, and he told it correctly. However, the women in the audience, most of them M.B.A.s, were not amused. Some of them later let him know it, saying that they thought his sense of humor was insensitive and inappropriate. Given the circumstances, they were probably right.

If you insist on trying humor, make certain you abide by these four rules:

1. *Tell the story as if it were true.* The punch line is a lot funnier if we aren't expecting it.
2. *Tell the story to make a business point.* If you don't make a point, you have no business telling a joke.
3. *Never tell a story at the expense of women or minorities.* If you do, you will surely regret it. You will likely be cast ever after as a bigot and boor, and perhaps even trigger a self-inflicted career setback.
4. *Make sure you tell the story correctly, and don't mess up the punch line.*

9

FORGING A
POWERFUL MESSAGE

—— *O* STANDS FOR ONE THEME ——

Winston Churchill—arguably the greatest speaker of the last century, but almost forgotten today—said that you can't talk about more than one thing at a time. This is particularly true when you are just one of a series of speakers at a meeting or event. It is tough enough to try to remember what everyone said if all six play the game correctly and each one has only one message. You've still got half a dozen concepts to try to digest.

But the reality is always worse. The reality is that each speaker will very likely *not* know how to play the game and will try to cram a lot of information into a very small space—without thought to what is the larger truth, what is the real message. These people will try to talk about more than one thing at a time. What I'm saying is that it is never enough to simply catalog information and present it to your audience on a tray.

It is never enough simply to rattle off a list of things you want to say. The only way to talk about many things (and transform information into knowledge) is to make them all sound like one thing. To do that, you begin by taking a position. Figure out the need, change, or trend, and then present your case from *that point of view*. Your point of view will give you your theme.

Let us say you have determined that your theme is globalization. When we translate globalization into a simple sentence, we come up with something like: "The future of our company depends in part on our ability to plug into the global economy." Fine. Now we have globalization translated into a business message coupled with a real sense of urgency. That's a big subject full of possibilities and more than enough to talk about in the next eighteen minutes or so.

Now you might argue that while it is all right to talk about globalization, you also want to talk about a lot of other things that affect your business. My answer is that you may certainly discuss all these items, as many as you like—as long as you *clearly link every subtopic to the original overriding concept* of globalization. So if you must talk about research and development, for example, under the principles of the POWER formula you could only discuss research and development as it relates directly to globalization. Research and development would then become an aspect of globalization, as would strategic planning, marketing, advertising, and all the rest.

In Chapter 13 we will talk about the two varieties of theme—the rocket and the necklace—but first, let's open the windows.

10

TALKING
WITH PICTURES

―――― *W* STANDS FOR WINDOWS ――――

In our model, a *window* is a way to see inside the presentation. Windows represent concrete examples.

A strong message *without specifics to back it up* is a bankrupt message. Every proposition needs proof for credibility. To provide credibility, we have to build in windows—concrete examples, pertinent illustrations, proper data, anecdotes, or analogies that provide the flip side to the concept.

A concept is only an abstraction, and abstractions are about as easy to remember as a dream after waking. Every idea linked to a theme must have a solid example, a window, linked to the idea—because we know from experience that concepts that try to stand alone fall alone. They go in one ear and out the other. So it is not a good use of an audience's time to endure a string of abstractions—

and the problem is only compounded if subsequent speakers make the same mistake.

Ernest Hemingway said: "Don't tell me about it—show it to me." That's how he wrote. He *showed* you the matador dying in the bloodied sand of the bull ring, and then let you see what death was like through the matador's own eyes. Hemingway *showed* you what fear was like as German soldiers stormed stone walls. That's what you've got to do. *You've got to build little word pictures and give solid information.*

To say you had a "great year," for example, has no real value, no credibility. Why a great year? How? Compared to what? Measured in what way? On what do you base your claim? The basis for the claim is more interesting than the claim itself because specific examples are always more interesting.

So tell them about the surprising turnaround in sales in the southeast, for example—up more than 50 percent over the last year. Or about the favorable article in *BusinessWeek*, or how your trip to China produced a bonus order of 20 million units for the Chinese market.

Failing to provide your audience with examples is like a lawyer presenting a case in court but forgetting to provide evidence. Your "evidence" as a speaker is the *examples you pull up to prove your case.* If our topic is globalization and our subtopics are strategic planning, research and development, quality control, management development, and so on, then let's add another dimension—another level down—that gives weight to the subtopics and is made up exclusively of relevant examples. Put another way, the examples modify the subtopics, and the subtopics modify the theme. We include nothing extra, no tangents, and no distractions.

To illustrate further, if you were pressing your case and arrived at the part where you were explaining the vital link between strategic planning and global achievement, you would now want to begin giving interesting examples of what you mean. You might mention, for instance, a case history of a company that executed a certain strategy successfully and came up with interesting results. Conversely, you could talk about another company that failed to have any apparent strategy at all—and got crushed. Or you could offer a "what-if"—present a hypothetical case that paints a positive or negative view to reinforce your point.

Just remember that it will profit you little to prepare carefully, present eloquently and articulately, and be in complete command of your subject if your audience doesn't get nor remember what you said. Too often we believe, wrongly, that just because we understand, other people understand. To really help people not only understand but remember months later, we should shower them with examples.

The bottom line here is that a presentation with no examples, a presentation that sounds more like a white paper or an academic thesis, is *no presentation at all.*

11

THE CONVERSATIONAL APPROACH

—— *E* IS FOR EAR ——

Make sure you speak in ordinary language. Resist the temptation to talk in the "secret handshake" and "memo" language of your business or discipline. The toughest three feet of your life can be simply the transition from talking sitting down to talking standing up. Many of us seem to speak more formally and less conversationally on our feet than we do sitting down. In other words, we stop being ourselves and start presenting. For most people, that stylistic difference means a marked slide in effectiveness. The trick is to be consistently conversational whether sitting down or standing up.

> We are always at our best when we are ourselves, speaking *conversationally* in everyday, ordinary language. Whatever barriers exist between you and your audience can vanish when you talk the way you *normally* talk.

Earlier, I mentioned the idea of barroom talk—in which you picture yourself in a bar with friends or in a similar situation where performance anxiety virtually vanishes. In this zone of comfort you are more likely to find yourself and be yourself. Barriers weaken, fear disappears, and the real you emerges. This is the only person in the world you can ever count on to get you closer to customers, employees, peers, investors, senior management, and decision makers.

Stop thinking that every time you stand up to say something you are making a speech—because you're not. What you're really doing is having an enlarged conversation—even though there may be a hundred people listening and even though you may be doing all the talking.

You always have a choice when you enter into a dialogue or communication of any kind: you can clarify or you can obfuscate. Sometimes people obfuscate without realizing it. But some people, for lots of different reasons, actually obfuscate on purpose.

The acknowledged master of incomprehensible language is the seasoned bureaucrat—a wily creature who has been known to devote his entire working life to dodging responsibility and remaining almost totally faceless, forgettable, and invisible—all of which requires a considerably developed repertoire of verbal camouflage. An experienced bureaucrat can raise the art of obfuscation to ingeniously ambiguous new heights.

Take, for example, the venerable Alan Greenspan, onetime chairman of the Federal Reserve Board. Greenspan and other Fed chairs before him have had a long tradition of cryptic allusion in public commentary, which allows them to hint at future action without feeling obliged to actually take any action. Here's what Greenspan told Congress:

GREENSPAN: *"Our monetary policy strategy must continue to rest on ongoing assessments of the totality of incoming information and appraisals of the probable outcomes and risks associated with alternative policies."*

TRANSLATION: *It's tough to set interest rates.*

GREENSPAN: *"When the Federal Reserve tightens reserve market conditions, it is not surprising to see some upward movement in long-term rates as an aspect of the process that counters the imbalances tending to surface in the expressionary phase of the business cycle."*

TRANSLATION: *The Fed's rate hike tanked the bond market because of fears of growth and inflation.*

GREENSPAN: *"Our long-run strategy implies that the Federal Reserve must take care not to overstay an accommodative stance as the headwinds abate."*

TRANSLATION: *We'll tighten some more.*

The IRS has proved itself consistently capable of taking bureaucratic fog to even more astonishing heights. Memos and reports—like books, newspaper articles, and speeches—*should always be written the way we speak*. With that in mind, consider this IRS proposal to improve the agency's security: "Complete validated Security Architecture; develop data encryption strategy and issue encryption Request for Proposal (RFP); pilot External Access Utility (EAU); prototype Audit Collection functionality."

Phew, no wonder millions of Americans can't get a straight answer from the tax collectors in Washington!

With the exception perhaps of bureaucrats, language tends to get simpler as you move up the ladder of any organization. In the boardroom the communication is typically straightforward, unpretentious,

> economical, and peppered with breezy, everyday clichés, which can arguably be a mistake in writing but serve as a kind of shorthand in speaking.

If you want to resonate, stick to *simple, straightforward, muscular Anglo-Saxon*. By contrast, many middle managers, who report to the people who work for the people in the boardroom, tend to go the other way, perhaps because they think they sound more professional. They cultivate the aforementioned corporate "secret handshake" language that is intended often to draw more attention to themselves than to what they are actually saying. At the middle management level, or what is left of middle management, it is sometimes possible to be lulled into a stupor by a mantra of swarming buzzwords.

The hidden agenda here is obvious, and only a reminder of the frailties of human nature. When middle managers salt their presentations with the insider language of a particular discipline, what they are really saying is, "Hey, pay attention to me! I'm a professional and I'd like to be appreciated."

So instead of saying, "We ought to spend more money on this idea in research and development," which is what you'd likely hear in the boardroom, the presentation two levels down might sound something like this: "Regarding the question of viability, it may indeed be necessary to interface with R&D in terms of measuring the projected relative scope of the product as it applies to the bottom line parameters of future sales, to impact our decision-making process in order to pro-opt a similar strategic move that could conceivably be undertaken by a near competitor. . . ."

This may be a tiny exaggeration to make a point, but I have actually heard and read worse. The irony is that senior managers are always grateful to hear presentations that are stripped of the burdensome language baggage they have to put up with every day. I know because they tell me so. Yet the further irony is that language changes won't be happening in a big way anytime soon. The reason is both psychological and cultural: most people measure their self-worth by the work they do, and they simply refuse to believe that larding presentations with quasi-intellectual, privileged language can be anything but rewarding. The self-conscious argot of the discipline only reinforces a notion of self-importance. It is a crutch, a prop that many people use for effect, much as they might an expensive suit— only in this case, it is at their own expense.

> Muscular, straightforward Anglo-Saxon is the language of leadership—and you can always count on it to serve you well.

To some degree, we are all guilty—lawyers, business managers, salespeople, marketing whizzes, engineers, teachers, and professors. Rather than prop us up, the language barriers we erect only serve as distractions, *leading us away from our objective of clarity* until we collapse under the weight of our own words.

Those who insist on business-speak or memo language to interact with other businesspeople, can expect by their own choice of words to be viewed as functionaries (the exception is when both parties are comfortable speaking in code as a kind of shorthand). By contrast, those who are seen as straight talkers are also seen as the leaders to whom the functionaries report. When push comes to shove, you can always count on straight talk to get the job done.

Recognizing an unmet need, in 2008 the entire McCain presidential campaign came down to just two words: *straight talk*. McCain lost, but the phrase resonated across party lines and attracted people from diverse ends of the political spectrum.

America's traditional corporate culture is only now beginning to recognize the business value of straight talk, led by a new generation emerging out of Silicon Valley and now evolving into what some people are calling the New Economy. But one top business leader was way ahead of his time.

Way back in the early 1980s, Chrysler Chairman Lee Iacocca went to Washington in a last-ditch effort to try to keep his company alive. Chrysler was threatened with bankruptcy, and Iacocca needed a lot of money fast. In the senate committee room where he was scheduled to present his case, he was accompanied by a battery of lawyers and what looked like a prepared text about three inches thick. The lawyers swarmed around Iacocca, but he brushed them aside and then shoved the fat text aside, too. He sat down behind the microphones, faced the senators, and said something like:

> *Gents, the situation is very simple. I've got 100,000 people who could be out of work in Michigan next week. Now, you can write them a check. We call that welfare, and these workers can go on the public dole. The taxpayer—your constituents—can pay for it.*
> *[Pause here—you can be sure he's got their attention.]*
> *Or you can write me that check, and I'll put these people back to work. We'll build the best cars in America, and we'll do it in just three years. Then I will personally pay back the money—with interest.*
> *And you can take that to the bank!*

The senators practically threw the money at Iacocca. A meeting that was scheduled to take half a day was over in twenty minutes. Iacocca got his money, the Chrysler Corporation had a new lease on life, and a lot of people kept their jobs. The government later got its money back on schedule with interest as promised, and everyone came out a winner.

You could argue that the only reason Chrysler exists today—the only reason you can still buy a Jeep Cherokee—is that its chairman had the good sense to go to Washington not sounding like a businessman.

The paradox here is that a businessman *should not sound like a businessman.* A chemical engineer should not sound like a chemical engineer. A lawyer should certainly not sound like a lawyer—and you can be sure that a consultant like myself should go out of his way not to sound like a consultant. I like to tell people that if I had a Ph.D. in communications, I probably wouldn't want them to know about it. Why? Because nothing gets in the way of doing business more than language that is anything other than conversational.

Ask anyone in business today, and they will tell you that most real business gets done *outside* the meetings—when we bump into people in the corridors, pick up the phone to bounce an idea back and forth, in snatches of conversation on the way to someplace else. In other words, real business gets done when we exercise our most consistently effective communications tool—*ourselves*. And we are only really ourselves when we are talking to people *naturally, conversationally*.

The real action comes down to face-to-face. I sometimes joke that's why God created golf. Ever wonder why CEOs often get automatic membership in golf clubs, paid for by their companies and shareholders? Because more deals are cut on the golf course every year than in all the conference rooms in the world.

12

THE STRONG FINISH

—— *R* STANDS FOR RETENTION ——

What do you want your audience to do? *Retention* for our purposes means strong ending. It is as necessary to have a strong ending as it is to have a strong beginning. After all, this is the last thing you will be saying, so it only makes sense to make the last thing memorable. Don't forget that you want your audience not only to remember what you said but to actually go do what you want them to do. So your takeaway has got to be worth taking away. But first, I want to help you avoid a common trap: when you wrap it up, try *never* to say, "In conclusion . . ." or "In summary . . ." or "To conclude . . ." or "To summarize . . ."

Why? Because if you do, your language sends a signal that you are making a *presentation,* not having a *conversation* (you will hear more about this later). Of course, you are in fact making a presentation. But you should do everything in your power to *create the illusion that you are having a conversation*.

Can you see yourself in a bar saying to your buddy, "In conclusion . . ." or at home in the kitchen with your significant other saying, "So dear, in summary . . ."? Probably not.

The conversational alternatives are as follows:

- "So it all comes down to this . . ."
- "Put it all together and here's what we've got . . ."
- "So here's the message . . ."
- "Bottom line . . ."

Now let's look at seven ways to end strongly:

1. Summarize your key point or key points. One or three, but not two or four, because the ear likes the odd number (two anticipates three) and four is too many to remember.

This means you could restate your main message and then perhaps give three reasons to back it up. Or just give your main message and leave it at that. If you chose to give two main messages at the end, this would only serve to divide at the very moment you should be unifying. **Best rule of thumb:** *Stick with one big message.* For example: "So our future, as you can see, lies in our own hands. It is not too late to correct our mistakes and to recognize that our success will depend on our determination and ability to expand rapidly into the global marketplace."

2. Loop back to the beginning. Let your ending echo your start. This technique is not only intellectually satisfying and in a design sense aesthetically pleasing, but it can also save time in preparation. That's because if you are in a hurry, once you figure out what your theme is, and you can synthesize that theme into simple language, then your theme can become not only your bottom line (the last words) but also the top line (the headline, the first words). As before, alpha becomes omega, and vice versa.

Of course, you can do the same with virtually any of the eight ways to start strongly, which we discussed earlier. So at the end you would reach back to your beginning and pull up the personal story, illustration, strong statement, quotation, rhetorical question, look at the past or future, or any variety of these as a closing. Naturally, you would want to couch the retelling in different words so it didn't sound like you were memorizing a spiel off a tape in your head.

For example, you might say:

> *My hope, then, is that if we do our jobs right, I might be able to find on my next visit to London that our products are on the shelves not only at Harrods, but every other department store, as well . . . and in France and Germany and Italy and eventually even in Eastern Europe. And I see another day soon when those cash registers will begin to ring again at Bloomingdale's and all over this country; then all over the world—when people are buying* [product X] *from Seattle to Singapore and from New York to New Delhi.*

This could be a new CEO with a new worldwide strategic plan talking to her own troops for the first time. By referring back to the Harrods and Bloomingdale's anecdote, she has reminded everyone that she is on top of the problem and has a solution.

3. Call for action: ask the audience to do something you want them to do. You can ask for permission to begin a project; ask for money from the board to pay for that project; ask for help, endorsement, ideas, cooperation, authority, consensus—anything. As any good salesperson will tell you, sometimes if you don't ask, you don't get. Sometimes you don't even get the order if you don't ask for it.

A politician will often ask for help, or the vote. An evangelist might present his case (you're going to Hell) and then ask you to accept God. A senior corporate officer chairing a meeting of disparate and perhaps competing elements of the same company might demand cooperation and ask for consensus. The head of a nongovernment organization (NGO) might make an appeal for financial support to her audience like this:

> *So I'm asking you to join with us today—right now—to try to help make a better life for so many with so little. I'm asking you to write the check and to write your congress person and senator,*

to use the power of your voice and your vote to help make the world a better place.

4. Appeal to the positive. If a situation is not favorable, seek whatever good news you can and put a good face on an otherwise not encouraging story. As a matter of course, we often overlook the occasional pieces of gold buried in all the gravel we deal with every day. For example, if the dollar is weak, tourist travel overseas will be down, but so will our trade deficit because our products will cost less. If earnings were off again this year, that's bad. But if they were up from what they were last year, that's good. If we project that curve upward into next year and beyond, we could soon be making a lot of money again.

In business as in life itself we can choose to view setbacks either as obstacles or as stepping-stones. We can see a problem as a body blow or view it as a challenge. We can complain and feel sorry for ourselves and our situation, or we can look forward to the challenge of making it right.

Mistakes, challenges, obstacles, and setbacks all offer opportunities to sharpen skills, focus energies, stir the creative juices, think smarter, act faster, and perform better. The same is true for your presentation, not only in the preparation and delivery, but also in the message. Leave your audience with a sense of hope, a looking up and ahead at things rather than down and back.

For example, a beleaguered CEO talking to her own troops might wrap it up like this:

So I would ask you to forget about the bad news. Forget about what you see on TV and read in the newspapers. Stop listening to the naysayers and doom-and-gloomers. Dismiss the pundits and talking heads.

The reality is that everybody in this new industry is in the same boat, and we are all riding on the same tide. In our own company we have learned from our mistakes and we are better for it. Our balance sheet is getting stronger every day. We still have one of the most talented managements in the business, and we have positioned ourselves to profit on the rebound.

That's the message—tell your people.

5. Bad news/good news. The bad news/good news approach can defuse the potential for a hostile question-and-answer session in the event you see soft spots or loopholes in the case you are trying to make. For instance, a new CEO of a start-up might wind up his pitch to potential private equity investors like this:

It's true that we are new to this market, and it's true we have to move fast to meet our obligations and build out the business model in a challenging environment, and it's also true that regulatory concerns will continue to be an issue for the next several months.

But most important—and this is what I want you to take out of the room today—we are not only first to market, but in the twenty years I have been in the telecom wireless industry, I have not seen an opportunity with such rapid growth potential, long-term value, and return to investors.

Now you have released tension by anticipating their concerns. You might have also dodged some tough questions simply by acknowledging that these issues are on your radar and woven into your plan.

6. Project into the future. *Everybody loves a seer,* particularly in business and politics. The real news in most business presentations is not what happened yesterday or what's happening today, but what we can expect will happen tomorrow. That's the added value our presentation gives to senior corporate officers, who can base their decisions on what subordinates tell them. Those subordinates, in turn, base their projections on what happened, let's say, in the last couple of quarters. A division vice president who makes recommendations to a board's senior management committee based on intelligent projections, which themselves are the product of solid data, provides a good service. So the useful news should be what's coming.

If a big change in the demographics, say, of the customer base of a large insurance company is unfolding, then senior management will have to know about that change and take appropriate action. If federal legislation is in the works that would severely restrict or even ban the sale of a given product, then that information has got to take priority in any presentation relative to the endangered product. If the financials or sales and marketing numbers are developing into a pattern over recent quarters, that's important. You've got to know where those numbers are heading, what the changes mean for the business, and what we ought to be doing about them. Then you've got to project. You are now *translating* essentially random data into meaningful information that can have a measurable dollar effect on the company.

One reason so many business presentations fail is because they lack the added value of clear translation, mentioned earlier, and intelligent future projection.

I am talking about spotting trends and changes and vital signs, and then ending your talk in such a way that people hear and remember what you say and can take appropriate action, if necessary. Let's say, for instance, you are talking to a trade group and making the point that change is coming. You might end with something like this:

- "So based on everything we know, here's what I see . . ."
- "I see the recession softening and the dollar slowly strengthening . . ."

- ◆ "I see the Big Three growing again as early as this time next year . . ."
- ◆ "And I see new opportunities in Asia that weren't there just two years ago . . ."
- ◆ "Put it all together, and the next eighteen months could prove to be one of the most rapid periods of growth we have known since this industry began forty years ago . . ."

Note: *A good line to use for wrapping up any pitch ending with a projection is, "So where do we go from here?"*

7. Tell an allegorical story that embraces your theme. This can be difficult, and if not done correctly it may hinder more than help—because a story, if told self-consciously or without conviction, can sound precious and manipulative, even phony. So like humor, use of allegory can be *high* risk. But if executed skillfully in the right hands at the right time, there is *no better way to end*.

First of all, if you use a story you must pick one that hits the mark exactly, doesn't take too long to tell, and makes a clear business statement. The story you choose should also be timeless and serve as a kind of fable. For example, if you are making the point that your company must build a first-rate marketing team to compete in the global economy of the future, you could end this way:

When I think about the job ahead of us, I think of the lone traveler in the Middle Ages who came to a place where three people were working by the side of the road.

The traveler asked the first worker what he was doing, and the first worker said he was shaping rock.

The traveler asked the second worker what he was doing, and the second worker answered that he was building a wall.

Then the traveler asked the third man, and the third man explained that he was building a cathedral. [pause]

Well, in a similar sense, while we're not exactly building cathedrals, I think it's fair to say that we're trying to take the

longer view—to create something of enduring value that will
continue right into the next century.

Now you shut up. Your job is done and—if done with confidence
and conviction—done well. To add to that finish would only sub-
tract from the overall effect.

End with an image—an image, say, of a cathedral, to suggest
things lofty—and you give your audience the gift of a takeaway,
something they can remember six weeks later.

Remember: You are talking to people brought up on TV and video
games. When you speak, you yourself must in a sense become that
TV by telling stories and painting pictures.

At this point, you have armed yourself to take on even the most
challenging speaking assignment. But first, let's take a look at what
we've created:

P Punch. Strong start (begin with the ending, personal story,
illustration, rhetorical question, quotation, past, future, humor).

O One theme. One message (plus subthemes linked to main
theme).

W Windows. Specific examples to back up your main theme.

E Ear. Speak conversationally. Avoid business-speak.

R Retention. End strongly (summary, loop, call for action, positive view, bad news/good news, projection, story).

You may use as many starting methods as you wish, and the
same goes for your ending. You may start with a personal story followed by a strong statement, followed by a rhetorical question, for

example. And you may end with a repeat of your main point, plus your appeal to the audience, followed by a story.

The POWER formula is not just a tool kit. It is also a universal POWER tool. Plug it into any speaking assignment. Watch your preparation time melt away, leaving you free to do other things. Watch your audience look at you with new interest, wide awake, and responding. Watch your POWER go up—way up, while the time it takes to make the presentation goes down. Watch people remember not only the message but even the details. Watch them remember you, too. And watch them take action.

Now it's time to pump POWER into your *rocket* and blast off.

13

GETTING THE
MESSAGE ACROSS

—— THE ROCKET ——

The CEO of a big consumer products company was preparing for his annual meeting and announced that he had eight important points he wanted to cover. I explained that this would have been counterproductive, because people can't retain more than one idea at a time. So we redesigned the approach. In the end, he wound up with just a single message. But he was still able to make all eight points—because we positioned each point as a part of one overriding theme. In other words, all the points were just another way of expressing the message.

The design I am talking about is what I call the *rocket*.

Picture every talk, lecture, speech, conversation, or presentation as a rocket ship—a design elegantly simple, yet manifestly functional. The rocket is designed with minimum air drag, moves very fast, is usually aimed at a target, has a lot of power, and can pack a terrific payload.

If more business presentations were designed like rockets, we would waste a lot less time and get a lot more done.

Visualize a rocket. In the nose cone you have your all-important message, your theme, which you will launch into the heads of everyone in the audience. Now picture design lines in the fuselage of the rocket, which lead from the "warhead" directly down into the body of the ship. At the ends of those design lines are subtopics. Each is connected to the nose cone, and each serves as a kind of separate fuel pod to power the rocket on its way.

We know that we can't try to talk about more than one thing at a time. But if we want to talk about a lot of things, that's all right, too—*as long as each subject is linked directly to our larger theme.* In other words, each subject is just another aspect of the big message. This leaves no room for tangents and discourages redundancies.

—— DON'T SWITCH GEARS ——

The key to getting the biggest bang out of the rocket is to avoid making the mistake everyone else makes. You will often hear people say, "Now I'd like to switch gears . . ." or "Now I would like to move on and discuss . . ." or "Let me turn now to something else . . ." Suddenly your audience gets the incorrect impression that you have five, six, seven themes. Do that, and all could be lost. This can be a *fatal* error and must be avoided.

Without your guidance, audiences don't know which newly introduced subject may be your theme. Worse, let's say you are just one of many speakers at a two-day event, and all the other presenters make the same mistake of trying to talk about half a dozen points separately with no effort to connect them as one voice. Then instead of perhaps eight or ten messages, suddenly we are dealing with fifty messages. This is clearly unproductive. Themes melt into the muck, and you can't blame all the people who complain later that they thought the whole thing was a waste of time. So if you want people to remember what you say, and you respect the fact that they took the time to come to hear you say it, then you'd better start thinking rocket.

If your theme is the need for globalization, but you also want to talk about research and development, strategic planning, productivity, profitability, sales and marketing, and manufacturing, you might try weaving your subthemes into your main theme like this:

- ◆ "We can't talk about globalization without talking about the challenges of distribution on a global scale . . ."
- ◆ Or, "So we will be a global enterprise, but to do that we've also got to be smart and that's where strategic planning comes in . . ."
- ◆ Or, "In a global marketplace, nobody can compete without higher productivity, and that's why we are spending more than 100 million dollars this year alone to streamline our processes and upgrade our manufacturing facilities . . ."

Put it all together, and the design of your rocket may look something like this:

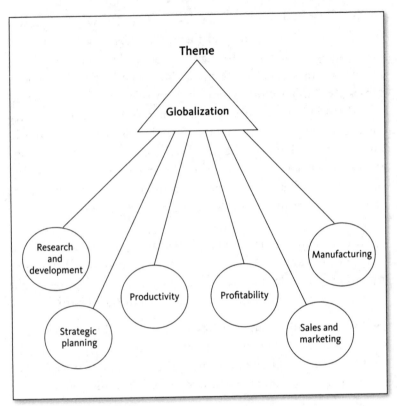

If you were to try to talk about these subjects in a random manner, you would wind up with a random presentation—a presentation of six themes (seven, if you include globalization)—seemingly going nowhere. But by unifying them under a kind of central command, you have turned a jellyfish into a potent missile that you can be sure will have an impact. One of the beauties of shaping your concepts in the form of a rocket is that the rocket is a unified instrument of pure intellectual energy.

All its working parts are strategically connected for maximum impact. Pick any part of our model rocket, and you can't have one part without the other. In a sense, the parts act in concert, like a team: one for all and all for one.

Consider, for a moment, the POWER formula and our presentation that has globalization as its theme. We have talked about how research and development, strategic planning, productivity, profitability, sales and marketing, and manufacturing all relate to globalization. Now let's go one more step and give concrete examples to back up our position (remember that examples are the *W* in *POWER*). Add the examples, and the design looks like this:

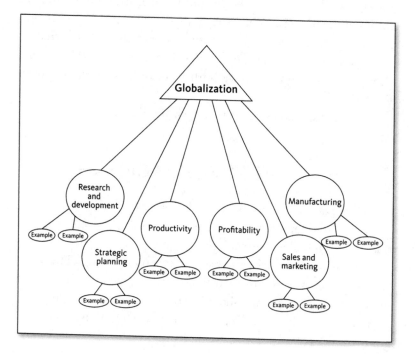

Aside from the remarkable simplicity of the model, three points should come immediately to mind:

1. The rocket has an actual rocket shape. It's streamlined with all the parts fitting together in a very functional way.
2. Everything is headed in the same direction.
3. Everything is connected.

This last point is vitally important. Profitability is discussed only in the context of globalization, and examples are offered only to reinforce profitability. Break that rule at any point in a presentation, and the presentation itself will start to lose shape and eventually fall apart.

So you could say that *POWER* is to organization as *rocket* is to streamlined design. The key to getting the biggest bang out of the rocket is to make *POWER* appeal to the mind. *Rocket* appeals to the mind as well, but also to the curious but enduring notion that all things are really one. When you apply this principle to a presentation, everything—*everything*—in that presentation is connected.

In other words, rocket and POWER are two aspects of the same thing. At this point we have built a rocket and packed it with POWER.

Now you should be ready to launch at will.

—— THE NECKLACE ——

If you have no subthemes, then you do not have a rocket. Nor do you need one. Without separate categories embedded in your presentation, then you will want to design a *necklace*. The necklace is simply one message with examples to back up that one message. The necklace is the most straightforward and effective way to capture the mind of your audience and should be the method of choice for business presenters. Fast, moving, powerful presentations are almost always necklaces.

> Necklaces quickly establish a position and then thrust
> ahead to prove the thesis with one piece of compelling
> evidence after another.

A skillful presenter can use the necklace to change behaviors and stir action—whether you are General George Patton inspiring his troops, Barack Obama confronting the race issue in a historic speech to the American people, or a salesperson selling goods and services to a prospective client.

The effectiveness of the necklace and its beauty both lie in its *simplicity*. Picture a necklace. The necklace is silver thread strung with pearls. The silver thread is your theme. The pearls are examples that hang on the theme. Unlike with the rocket, there are no subthemes. The necklace becomes complete when you attach the two ends together and it forms a circle.

For centuries, historical figures of every stripe—politicians, kings, emperors, and others—have used the necklace to spur action: join the revolution, charge into battle, even to persuade people to give up their lives for a cause. In our own time, extremists of the cloth seem to have a particular talent for putting the necklace to violently productive (read *destructive*) use. Radical Muslim clerics, for example, have no trouble bending vulnerable minds to dastardly deeds. Osama Bin Laden is a master of the necklace:

- **Silver cord:** Protect Islam from the infidel.
- **Pearls:** A litany of perceived humiliations and injustices and a call to jihad.
- **Result:** 9/11, jihad, and an endless conga line of suicide bombers.

I remember a professor in college who waxed rhapsodic for fifty-five minutes about the Ralph Waldo Emerson journals and Emerson's passion for nature. The rhetoric was eloquent, but the lecture was thin on examples, which made it tough for us students to stay with the professor for more than eighteen minutes. Today I can remember very little from that course, whereas I am happy to say I can recall much more from courses in which the instructors were wise enough to use illustrations, either verbal or pictorial. The professor had a silver thread, but few pearls—not a good necklace. So he missed a chance to give us a rich learning adventure, and we missed the opportunity to get one.

By contrast, I remember watching a film clip of an American evangelist in the Philippines. A stadium was filled with 30,000 people. His theme was clear—maybe the most depressing theme ever: *You are all going to Hell!*

Then he whipped out his Bible and started throwing out parables (pearls)—Ezekiel and the wheels of fire, Daniel in the lion's den, the miracle at Cana, the prodigal son, the good Samaritan, the sermon on the mount, Revelations, and so on—positioning each pearl to support the theme. If you expect to dodge Hell, you'll need grace, redemption, salvation. He was so effective, 6,000 people came forward to sign up. That's a big number by any sales or marketing measurement. In the right hands, the necklace can deliver the same kind of results in business.

The necklace's *secret of success* is that all the wood gets behind the arrow—a relentless barrage of compelling evidence that finally overwhelms the listener.

Say, for example, you've got a problem because your division is lagging expectations, and you need to rally the troops with a call to arms. Your theme is that recent industry-wide setbacks have positioned the division to outflank the competition when the recovery commences. That's your silver cord.

Now you provide proof with pearls:

- New products in the pipeline (Name names.)
- Increased research and development spending (How much? Which products?)
- Ramped-up marketing and advertising campaigns (Which brands? Where? How?)
- Hiring of top talent (Who?)
- New partnerships (Which?)
- Divestments of losing brands (Which losing brands?)
- Sustainable revenue strategy (How does it work?)
- Greater projected market share (How much greater?)
- Customer service overhaul and upgrade (What kind of overhaul and upgrade?)
- New trouble-shooting "SWAT teams" in the field (How will they troubleshoot?)

Then straight to a strong ending and you are done.

When I tell people their presentations are too long, the typical reaction is, well, we'll just take out a few examples. Bad idea. That's like throwing out the evidence, or tossing the baby out with the bathwater. The better solution is to edit, streamline, avoid redundancies, and actually *add* examples (which parallels the point we made in the window part of POWER).

This exercise of edit and redesign cuts fat and adds sparkle, with the result that the pitch is shorter and delivers with impact—because the audience now gets the right information in the right way. Ultimately, this transition translates into measurably higher productivity for everybody involved, speaker and audience alike.

The POWER formula, the rocket, and the necklace are your guarantees that your time, work, and effort will not go unrewarded. By themselves, these tools can go a long way to making sure that when it comes your turn to speak, you will not be making the same mistakes as your peers.

Add the rocket and the necklace to POWER and you get:

THE POWER FORMULA

Punch

1. Begin with the ending (strong statement)
2. Personal story
3. Anecdote or illustration
4. Quotation
5. Rhetorical question
6. Project into future
7. Look into past
8. Humor (tell as if true, make business point, be appropriate, and don't blow punch line)

One Theme (Rocket or Necklace?)
One message, one mission, one theme only. But you may discuss that one theme in many different ways.

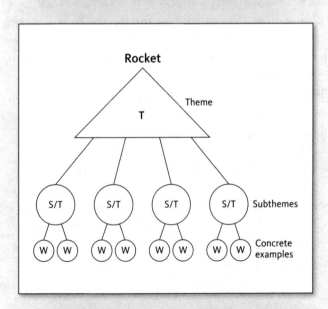

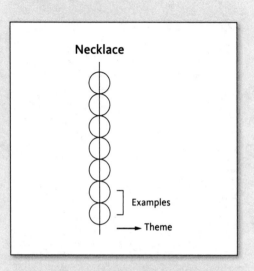

Window
Specific examples, illustrations, and anecdotes to provide proof. (This is how you let audiences actually see inside your presentation.)

Ear
Stay conversational. Don't speechify.

Retention
1. Summarize key point
2. Loop back to beginning
3. Call for action
4. Appeal to the positive
5. Bad news/good news
6. Project ahead
7. Tell a symbolic story that embraces your message

PART THREE

DELIVERY

14

THE 18-MINUTE WALL
Audience Attention Span

A LL YOUR PLANNING, talents, and good execution will be in vain if you fail to recognize one simple—and critical—law of nature.

In the 1970s the U.S. Navy did a study to find out how long people can listen to other people talk. The objective was to best use the time of instructors and students throughout the Navy's education system. The answer surprised a lot of people. The answer was not an hour nor even half an hour. The answer was just eighteen minutes. The Navy found that in a classroom, presentation, or lecture environment, an audience's ability to focus on what the speaker is saying and then remember what was said drops off at eighteen minutes like the continental shelf plunging straight down into the abyss. Unhappily, very few people today are aware of that study or the resulting vital number. If they were, we would save tens of millions of wasted hours and untold lost productivity in business in the United States every year.

But what if we are unable, for any number of different reasons, to limit what we must say to eighteen minutes? In real life, particularly in business, we find that presentations often go longer than eighteen minutes. Frequently we see, for example, board presentations, analyst presentations, and new business presentations running forty minutes or longer—and it's not uncommon that a presentation can sometimes take an entire morning or afternoon, and even on rare occasions, a full day.

Change the medium to break the tedium.

I see five ways to get around the 18-minute wall:

1. Go to Q&A (question and answer). Cover the basics, all the essentials, in fifteen minutes, and then set aside thirty minutes for Q&A to touch on details and elements that you feel might need further explanation or fleshing out. Q&A, by the way, is your chance to redeem yourself if you feel that the presentation itself did not go particularly well. Most of us tend to be more effective in Q&A, anyway, because Q&A allows us to be most ourselves and most conversational. We can establish a more personal rapport with the audience and reinforce positions that contribute toward whatever objective we may have—whether it is seeking endorsement, demanding a plan of action, enlisting help, or asking permission.

2. Use another speaker. Have an associate speak for two minutes or so to highlight, clarify, or amplify a particular area of expertise; then the clock starts again with you. You may repeat the process before the next eighteen minutes are up, but human nature probably wouldn't allow you to use the strategy successfully a third time. Alternatively, you can bounce back and forth from speaker A to speaker B—as long as both of you and the presentation appear to be seamless and unrehearsed.

3. Invite questions and be prepared to interact with your audience. You might even start off with a question, such as: "When was the last time you asked yourself, 'Where will I be in five years?'" or "Where do you think your company will be in six months?"

The downside here is that you can't let the conversation get out of control. To pull it off, you've also got to be a good facilitator, such as Charlie Rose of PBS or the hosts of shows like "Meet the Press," to get the conversation back on track and back on point.

4. Show a video. Bring along a DVD, CD, flash stick, or videotape that shows, for example, your company at a glance, a new manufacturing process, a new research facility going up, a news clip pertinent to the issue at hand, or clips of other speakers—and insert the video into your presentation at the appropriate time. (This is often not an option for people in financial services.) The video can run up to ten minutes or so and be a nice addition to your presentation. Then you can safely continue to talk for another eighteen minutes.

5. Tell a business story a minute. Borrow a tip from the masters. Tell one anecdote after another to drive home your theme—a personal recollection, something you saw on TV or read in the newspapers, something somebody told you. This is how evangelists can command a stage alone for two hours—because they are talking about a subject that is perceived to be of vital interest by like-minded audiences, using apt illustrations to vividly underscore a single message.

15

HOW TO CAPTURE
YOUR AUDIENCE

—— TWO BIG 8s ——

The 8-second rule will ensure that you always get off to a good start. Mastering the 8-second drill can help make you a player in no time.

The 8-Second Rule

Keeping the important 18-minute wall in mind, we now have to consider the fast start *8-second rule*. The 8-second rule recognizes a law of human nature that suggests that most people decide within eight seconds whether a particular speaker is worth listening to in the first place. In other words, don't piddle away your moment of greatest impact on opening amenities. Opening amenities are opening inanities.

So begin with a *bang*. Avoid anemic cliché starts such as, "Thank you. Good morning. It is a pleasure to be here today. . . . Today I would like to talk about. . . ." As we have been saying, most presenta-

tions, talks, lectures, and speeches—an overwhelming majority—
do begin that way. But that's not a good reason to do so ourselves. In
fact, one way we can distinguish ourselves is through our *uniqueness*.
Good managers value differences even in a team environment. Who
will criticize us for being different if being different means we can
also be more effective?

No one will fault you for saying, "Thank you." That's fine.
"Thank you" is cordial. But skipping the thank you and getting
right at it is, in my view, even better.

The 8-Second Drill: The Shorter the Better

Of all the virtues that a good speaker brings to the party, none is
more highly prized than *brevity*. More than a century ago, Mark
Twain got a telegram from a publisher. The telegram read: "Need
2-page short story, two days." Twain wired back: "No can do 2 pages
two days. Can do 30 pages two days. Need 30 days to do 2 pages."

> Shorter is sometimes harder. But shorter is also usually better,
> because it concentrates essential information into a narrower space,
> thereby casting a brighter light on the subject and cutting down the
> time we need to listen.

The ability to focus information into ever-smaller time slots is a
skill *essential* to our time. For example, a friend of mine was
summoned to his boss's office for a meeting that was supposed to
take about half an hour. But as my friend got off the elevator, he
found his boss heading for another elevator, beckoning my friend to
join him.

Something urgent had come up, the boss explained. My friend
now found himself having to distill a half hour into the twenty seconds it took the elevator to reach the ground floor. He had to figure

out his bottom line, edit and review it in his mind to make sure he left nothing out and added nothing extraneous, and then sum it all up crisply, clearly, and with confidence. Happily, this was no problem because he had already worked with me in sessions to sharpen his powers of concentration on demand and under pressure.

The 8-second drill in a conversation about nuclear weapons in the post–Cold War period might be:

> *The most dangerous single threat to civilization is the spread of atomic bomb technology and other weapons of mass destruction to Islamic extremists and the Third World.*

The 8-second drill about a local pollution problem might be:

> *Our river is dying. We have got to take action now to save it— before it's too late.*

Interestingly, when people have experienced the 8-second drill in a training session—driving from three minutes down to eight seconds—they become amazed at how many unnecessary words they commonly use to talk about even the simplest subjects. They are even more surprised when they try to reverse the process—pushing back out to three minutes from eight seconds—often finding it is actually difficult to go beyond forty seconds.

The 8-second drill is an exercise my clients experience in the course of their leadership communication coaching. But anyone can practice the 8-second drill at home. Here's how it works:

1. Pick a timely or pressing business topic to talk about for three minutes. Take a position. Have an opinion. Don't just narrate a list of facts, a historical chronology, or a loose set of concepts without evidence to back them up. For example, instead of talking about "Globalization in the next century," talk about "Our survival as a nation may depend on our ability to dominate global markets in the next century." That's a position.

2. Present your case. Write down some ideas. Set up a logical course to follow. Detail the steps you plan to take; then set your notes aside. With your ideas all in a row and fresh in your head, stand in front of a mirror or a portable TV camera and start talking. Allow yourself not even one second more than three minutes.

3. Now take one minute off your time, and do the same thing in two minutes. Then go to one minute, thirty seconds, twenty seconds, ten seconds, and finally eight seconds.

—— GRACE UNDER PRESSURE ——

One of my clients, whose name happens to be Grace, found herself unable to land in Bangkok because of violent monsoon weather. She'd been sent from New York by her firm to make a presentation to civic and business leaders in Thailand for a contract worth tens of millions of dollars. By the time her plane landed two days late, other firms had made their pitches. The Thai officials had pretty much made up their minds and were reluctant to see her. Finally, a committee agreed to meet with her, for twenty minutes only, in a hotel lobby.

Any hope of a proper presentation went out the window. She knew she had to abandon her original game plan. Forget the deck and the PowerPoint. Forget the carefully groomed script. Now it was quick thinking, mental discipline, rapid regrouping and reorganization, streamlining, editing, and refining. Everything had come down to just a few minutes face-to-face with a bunch of complete strangers.

All this with a case of jet lag that made her feel like she'd been up for two days—and she had, almost. She felt oddly tipsy, a little punchy. But the stakes were too high to yield to sloppy thinking. The company's immediate future and her career, she knew, hung in the balance. She shrugged off the jet lag, cleared her head, and forced herself to focus.

When the Thai leaders arrived in the lobby, they were courteous but refused to sit down. They were letting her know that they were in a hurry and that the meeting would have to take place standing. To press the point, they glanced at their watches. It was all over in fifteen minutes (originally, she had planned to speak for an hour or more). When they were gone, she sank into a lobby chair and worried that it had gone badly.

The following day she flew home—but not before learning to her surprise and delight that she had won the account, over seven other vendors! To this day, she attributes the secret of that success and many more that followed to her familiarity with and skillful execution of the 8-second drill.

The hardest part is from thirty seconds on down. When you get to twenty seconds, you are in the neighborhood of the typical eighteen-second "sound bite" broadcasters talk about. Ten seconds is a real crunch, and eight seconds is about as far as any human being can reasonably be expected to go.

When you finally break through to eight seconds, you will have captured the *absolute essence* of what you are talking about. This single statement, phrase, or idea embraces your theme. It is your message. Frequently, when people tell me they don't know what their theme is, I tell them to try the 8-second drill. Your message, whatever it may be, cannot hide in the spotlight of the 8-second drill. If you don't already know your bottom line, you can be sure it will reveal itself every time.

If you want to have some fun, ask someone to time your performance and help you work your way all the way down to the 8-second prize.

Put the 8-second drill to good use next time you run into the unexpected—for example, at an important business meeting, and suddenly have to throw your carefully crafted plans out the window and reverse the wave.

The 8-second drill tells us that we could all be a lot crisper. Crispness makes important information easier and quicker to give, easier to get, and a lot easier to retain. Crispness saves time, enhances productivity, helps leaders lead, and can be the catalyst that transforms mere information into knowledge.

—— REVERSING THE WAVE ——

The 8-second drill is a function of "reversing the wave"—that is, getting to the point right away. Some lawyers, accountants, salespeople, and others are accustomed to taking their time to explain themselves by typically building to an elegant conclusion (slowly advancing toward their eventual message in the shape of a rising wave). If they are oblivious to the 18-minute wall and don't know how to get over it, they might drift unaware into treacherous territory and never know it.

When you "reverse the wave," you slash that risk by dashing to your message almost immediately. So if you are cut off or interrupted, or you unexpectedly run out of time, you can take comfort in the knowledge that your theme is already on the table. And if you are not cut off, you can relax a little and spend the rest of the time surfing down the back side of the (descending) wave and explaining how you came to your conclusion.

The 8-second drill makes it possible to know exactly how you should begin. More than that, it automatically defines three of the five functions of the POWER formula.

The top line (grabber)
The bottom line (message)
The last line (takeaway)

As you can see, it is simultaneously your strong start, theme, and ending.

Once you know the real point you're trying to make, then you can also *begin and end with that point* (leaders often recognize the advantages of this most basic form of reinforcement and explain what they want—a plan of action, for example—at the beginning as well as at the end). Start and finish are by definition the theme.

If we look at the globalization example mentioned a moment ago and apply the 8-second drill, the "top line" equals the "bottom line" equals the "last line." All the lines are one: "Our survival as a nation may depend on our ability to dominate global markets in the next twenty-five years." That's the hard nut that tells it all: big concept, few words. From this single line you can build a rocket ship or a necklace.

16

THE POWERPOINT PARADOX

Designing Visual Aids to Work for You—Never Against You

I F THE POWER formula is the architecture of the perfect presentation, visual aids (V/A) are the *foundation*.

At the senior level, visual aids are to be *avoided* whenever possible. In fact, I favor *restraint* at all levels. But V/A use is so widespread and so much in demand, and so many people depend on V/A as a crutch, that we might as well stop pretending that PowerPoint isn't in the room with us, and confront this 800-pound gorilla right now. Of all the chronic abuses systemic to the general mishandling of presentations, none is more consistently mishandled than PowerPoint.

PowerPoint is a big step up from the old days and not a bad idea. The problem is not PowerPoint itself, but the millions of people who don't know how to use it. In the right hands, it can do wonderful things and be an asset. The rest of the time, it is actually more of a problem than a solution. In the wrong hands, it allows us to go right on committing the same sins that we used to commit in the old days with overheads, transparencies, and slide projectors. Only now we can do it with a little more color, flair, and style. Take the not uncommon case of the expert who cratered.

—— THE EXPERT WHO CRATERED ——

I attended a corporate conference that featured an author and expert on "geoeconomics" who teaches at a well-known business school. Bad luck for him: he gets the slot right after lunch. But he loses no time making a bad situation even worse. First, he has the house lights turned off. Now we are in near total darkness. Right away, half the people in the audience can hardly keep their eyes open. With 400 well-fed attendees comfortably seated, endorphins are on a rampage and drowsiness is rapidly kicking in.

But rather than wake us up, our expert has hidden himself from view behind the lectern on the stage and buried his face in his script. On the screen is a PowerPoint slide filled almost entirely with words. Our expert is now reading these words, one by one. Three minutes later, he is still talking to the first word slide, but now he seems to be on a tangent. I've read the slide five times. I think he might be on the fifth of eight paragraphs. But I'm not so sure. I'm already bored, and at the moment I have no idea what he is talking about. I wonder how many others are in the same boat.

Another few agonizing minutes go by. We are all locked in a large room with the sandman, realizing too late how unproductive this is going to be. Those who are not nodding off are eyeing the exits. Several people have already slipped out. We are not even five minutes into this disaster.

Now appears a slide with four separate schematics and hundreds of numbers and words, just small enough that they can't be read, even from the front row. The good professor is droning on, but half the room is asleep, or just numb and keeping their eyes closed to shut out the pain and meditate on other things. More incomprehensible slides follow. Then more word slides. Is he reading or paraphrasing? What is this man talking about? What is he trying to say? Is it just me? Am I the dumbest kid in the class? Or am I having the same reaction as everyone else?

I am wondering, is this how this guy teaches his classes? Finally, I can take no more and slink up the aisle, out the door, and back into the light. Almost immediately, another escapee walks up and we begin to commiserate. A couple of other runaways and refugees wander over. It turns out that it's not just me, after all. We are all shaking our heads, trying to figure out what had just happened—or hadn't happened. The verdict is unanimous: smart man, dumb show. To add insult to injury—especially for the feckless souls who stuck it out—we later learned the presentation lasted an excruciating two hours.

Just another lesson in life about what can happen when we entrust our productivity to well-meaning people who just don't know any better. In this case, to be brutally candid, there wasn't even a hint of color, flair, or style. The ultimate irony came later that day when the professor, knowing I was an executive communications coach, approached me in a hotel lobby and asked me how I thought his presentation had gone.

I was at a complete loss for words. Finally, I said that it was one of the most extraordinary things I had ever seen and would probably never forget it. I made a couple of gentle suggestions, but he didn't seem pleased and wandered off.

—— TEN THINGS NEVER TO DO ——

An autopsy of the professor's embarrassing performance turned up the usual culprits. For the sake of economy, I will convert some of them into a short list of recommendations:

1. Don't turn off the lights—especially right after lunch.
2. Don't use word slides.

3. Don't allow your presentation to dominate.
4. Don't use slides no one can understand.
5. Don't get off track.
6. Don't bury your face in a script and read.
7. Don't take up people's time unless you have a message they can use.
8. Don't hide from your audience.
9. Don't speak for two hours—unless you know the rules of the game.
10. Don't make a mushy mess of what might have been an interesting story.

Back in the days when people relied on slide projectors and overhead transparencies the list of no-nos was long. Today, happily, it is shorter, and the rules have become simpler and much more straightforward.

You might be surprised just how simple they actually are:

1. *Begin and end with just you doing the talking.* In other words, don't begin or end your presentation with slides. Slides occurring simultaneously with a strong POWER start or ending are counterproductive. So stick all your graphs and pictures in the middle. This leaves you free to command the room with a strong start and strong finish.
2. *Dump all your word slides.* This does not mean they go away. It just means that instead of being on the screen or in the deck, they will now wind up only in the document, or hard copy.
3. *Introduce the next slide while the old slide is still up.* Don't advance to the next slide until you first prime the audience to what they are about to see.

Simple as pie. And as you will see, these rules make sense.

But I should note that for all their simplicity and proven effectiveness, even today these three easy rules often meet headwinds inside long-established, complacent organizations that have become culturally resistant to change.

THREE RULES FOR MAKING THE MOST OF POWERPOINT

Rule #1: The Oreo

The first rule is what I call the *Oreo*. Remember the POWER formula? The top layer of the Oreo represents your opportunity to launch a strong beginning. On the screen it's OK to show a logo or maybe your name, title, and logo—mental chewing gum that makes no demands. That's so the eye will not be distracted while you get off to your strong POWER start. It's just you and your personal story, anecdote, rhetorical question, or however you may choose to begin, and the logo on the wall. This lets you establish a tight and even personal relationship with your audience right from the start.

Now here's a neat little trick known only to the most successful and sophisticated speakers: make sure you tell your *entire* story before you show the first slide. Why? Because if something unforeseen creates an interruption or you run out of time, you will already have your cards on the table. People will know your entire story even if you are only a couple of minutes into your presentation (keep thinking *conversation* every time you see that dreaded word *presentation*). They will know your theme. They will know the challenges. And they will know the solutions. This is your insurance policy if things go wrong.

Assuming you do not run out of time or get interrupted, at some point you will say something like, "As you can see here . . ." or, "Take a look at this . . ." or, "So how do we know these things?" and click your remote to bring the first picture up on the screen.

The middle layer of the Oreo—the cream—is the graphics, tables, schematics, charts, and other visuals that help prove the theme. This is where you present the bulk of your evidence to make your case.

The bottom layer is your strong ending. When you are done presenting your visual supporting evidence (the cream), you will say something like (and this is worth repeating): "It all comes down to this . . ." or, "Put it all together and here's what we've got . . ." or, "So here's my message . . ." or, "Bottom line . . ." and click your remote for the last time. Up pops the same logo with your name that you used as your opening slide—the earlier top layer of your Oreo—and everybody is automatically back to paying attention to you and whatever you want to say. There is nothing more for them to look at because you took the visuals down, and now you are back in total control. This is an important moment. This is when you drive hard to your powerful finish.

So you are the top and bottom of the Oreo. You are the chocolate wafers. Strong on the top and strong on the bottom. The proof is in the cream filling (in this case, not in the pudding). Everybody loves Oreos, and everybody is going to love yours, too. This is always good news—particularly if your confection gets the order, sells the investor, or seals the deal.

Rule #2: Get Rid of Those Word Slides

If the word slides are gone, then what have we got? We've got charts, graphs, schematics, photos, and other visuals that are useful to support the theme—and that's *all* we've got.

The real estate on the wall is precious, and we need to use it *wisely*. We want to be 100 percent sure that *every* picture we show reflects, supports, and illuminates the theme—and the presenter. This leaves no room for word slides.

Toss the titles, agendas, and endless pages of whole sentences and paragraphs, even bullets (but save them for the digital or hard copy document). This is an important point and I will repeat it—word slides *do not* go away. They *remain* in the original presentation, which we will call the *document*. If you wish, you can use the document as a handout (only *after* the presentation), digital record, or reference source for Q&A.

So now you may wind up with a PowerPoint show on the screen that looks a lot different from the presentation full of word slides and excess data you started with. Most people rely heavily on word slides, so a sudden absence of word slides is likely to meet with loud objections. But word slides can be devastating. They are silent parasites that sap the life's blood out of your presentation—and you may never know it.

Think about word slides. A lot of people believe word slides double effectiveness and create reinforcement. They believe words on the screen make for a better show. But nothing could be further from the truth. In fact, word slides *slash* effectiveness and create *redundancy*.

But that's not the worst of it. Because the eye is so much more powerful than the ear, just give people an excuse to read words and sentences on a screen—and they will. This puts you in the awkward situation of having to compete with your own slides because people can't read and listen at the same time. Suddenly you are out of sync with your audience. At that point, you become a droning sound.

Under *no* circumstances should you allow your own show to reduce you to a background noise. You might as well not even be there. You could have saved yourself the time and effort and sent them a memo instead.

> If it's a competition between words you are saying and the written words they are reading on the wall, the words on the wall win hands down.

Even bullets can be a problem. I can read your bullets a lot faster than you can talk about each one individually. So while you are just finishing up with the first bullet, I have run down the list and now I want to move on. If I see that seven more bullets remain, like most people I will likely become impatient. And if you try to be cute about it—for example, showing me just one bullet at a time in a build—I will become outright antagonistic, because I can see how much more I've got to endure until we can get past this one slide. So word slides won't endear you to any audience. They can be particularly damaging if misused with an important group of decision makers you may be trying to get closer to or enlist. To make matters even worse, how many times have we been faced with endless word slides—only to realize that we can't even read the words because the letters are too small?

On top of that, word slides are a *serious liability* if you want to be seen as a leader, authority, or decision maker of any kind or even just be taken seriously. The signal you are sending when you share the room or the stage with word slides is that you are unable to discuss your own subject without cues. The audience assumes that without the word slides you would be lost, not knowing what to say, unsure of what's coming next, perhaps dependent on some junior person or colleague who prepared the show for you—when in fact, that may simply not be the case.

Your audience can't even be sure that the whole thing might not be corporate boilerplate right off the shelf. The hard truth is that anyone can do a boilerplate. I can do yours and you can do mine. All we have to do is read our lines. This means that from the audience's perspective, you might not be necessary as part of the value proposition. After all, we know from long experience that before your audience is willing to buy your product or service, or follow your lead, *first they have to buy you.* If you are not necessary or if you have made it too difficult for them to buy *you,* then what is your value?

Word slides and leaders do *not* mix.

In the end, word slides can drastically diminish whatever assets, such as talent, experience, wisdom, and intelligence, that you may carry with you into the meeting.

That's why many an expert comes off looking and sounding like an amateur, or why many a deal goes bad. Overuse of word slides can be a major contributor to negative outcomes for presentations of all kinds: sales, financial, new business, boardroom, and senior management, to name just a few.

Rule #3: Tell and Show

Rule #3 exists to make sure you control your presentation and your presentation does not control you.

Rule #3 says that it is smart to introduce the next slide before you show it, but not so smart to show it and then start talking about it. Why? Because if you start talking only after you can see your material, you are not in charge. Your word slides are in charge. You are obviously allowing your word slides to tell you what to say and when to say it, and this perception is to be avoided. You don't want your audience thinking that if the electricity went down, you would suddenly be at a loss for words.

What we are doing here, of course, is *tell and show,* not *show and tell.* The trick is to throw out an introductory line, perhaps just a single sentence that sets the stage for what is coming next. Let's call this the *roll-in.* Now let's assume that all those many word slides have been banished to the hard copy (document) where they belong and are no longer cluttering the screen, slowing you down, and generally mucking up your presentation. Your roll-in will tell us *in advance* what the business message is on the next slide (graphic)— even before we see that slide. This gives the perception that, like a good lawyer, you are introducing the jury to an idea and then revealing the evidence to back it up. This way, you are in control. You are making it clear that you don't need word slides to tell you what to say (in a moment we'll look at how to compensate for the loss of word slides).

How to create a *roll-in?* The roll-in essentially creates itself because it is always a brief summary of the business message, or the "takeaway," in the next slide, which itself amplifies and advances the central theme. So for example, if your theme is the need to go global, and the next slide shows domestic market share down compared to the same time last year, then your roll-in might be: "We got another reason to speed our global efforts just two months ago with the news that our market share is down more than 2 percent from last year."

Then *click* to the next slide. Pause for a beat to let everybody check the slide and get oriented. Then maybe draw their attention to last year's spike and this year's low, and point out that the projections, also depicted on the same slide, do not support further domestic efforts.

Let's say your next slide after that shows that sales and market share are both up in a Brazilian test market. So your roll-in to the next slide (while the current slide is still on the screen) might be, "By contrast, market share in Brazil is up almost double since we launched our first product just two months ago, as you can see here . . ." Then *click*. They now see exactly what you told them they would see. Both slides support the theme, as do the roll-ins.

At this point, many of you who have depended for years on word slides to provide guidance and help cut down on preparation time must be wondering how you can do without word slides and still pull off a good performance.

Actually, it's easy. You simply prepare a one-page "crib" sheet to serve as your private notes. Some people prefer to run little pictures of their slides down the left side of a standard 8-by-10 sheet of white paper. On the right, they might jot down their roll-ins to each one— just in case they forget. They typically keep this sheet nearby—on top of a stool, say, on an open stage, or at the podium, or in front of them in the conference room, so they can glance down and grab their cues. Ideally, if you really know your stuff, you may not even need a cue card.

Before we move on, I want to give you the exceptions to the rules governing slides.

—— EXCEPTIONS TO THE RULES ——

Exception to the rule that says you begin and end with just you talking: Sometimes for dramatic effect you might want to run (perhaps with music) a group of slides together before you even begin—a fast-moving cluster, say, of new products flashing across the screen, or snapshots of the new corporate headquarters, or images that suggest a new theme (such as sailboats racing against the wind or skydivers and climbers conquering the heavens and the mountains).

Or you might want to forget about slides and try a brief video with music for even greater impact. One of my clients opened an annual meeting of large corporate sales and marketing divisions by showing a Ferrari—engine screaming—rushing straight at the audience, then disappearing in a roar and a cloud of dust. The imagery was dazzling and set the stage for a fast-moving show. The message: things are changing quickly and we've all got to learn to win at ever-higher speeds. The added value of this very visual approach was that the client's presentation, the client, and the client's message all *stood out* from the run-of-the-mill grist ground out in forgettable presentations over the three-day conference period.

Exceptions to the rule that says no word slides: the larger the room, the more legitimate the argument for simple word slides—but no more than giant bullets. In an auditorium, say, it might make sense to throw up a huge one-word banner that reads:

PRODUCTIVITY

or

PROFITABILITY

so that people in the back rows a couple of hundred feet away, who may not feel as connected as the people up front or hear quite as well, can have a better idea of what's going on.

It also might make sense to show lists. For example, if you are talking about people, products, or services and can't—or won't—use photographs, then it is more efficient to show all the items together. For instance, suppose you highlight certain services or products but want to make the point that they are only part of a bigger picture. You mention a couple of key products and ask your audience to check out a list of all the others (just make sure the letters are big enough to be read in the back row). Then hit the clicker.

If you have some relevant excerpts from newspaper articles or apt quotes, you might want to enlarge them and put them on slides, as well. For example, you might want people to see a verbatim quote of a key player in your industry that may have a direct bearing on the point you are trying to make. To introduce the quote, you might say, "Few people saw any of this coming or understood what it meant. One who did was Jack Black, who had this warning for everybody in our industry. . . ." Then *click* to the quote.

Caution: The rule for using any "legitimate" word slide such as a quote is important. If you are going to ask people to read something, then you've got to shut up and give them a chance to read. There is no point in putting up a quote, for example, if you don't set it up with a proper roll-in and then pause for a few seconds to let the people absorb what you've said. This allows the meaning and implications of the written quote on the wall to fully sink in. Don't try to voice the quote aloud while they are trying to read it. Don't even try to paraphrase it. Just let it sink in. Then you can continue talking. Observing this critical moment of silence is the only way you can dodge the curse of redundancy and properly employ a word slide to create reinforcement.

When you drop the slide, you could "roll out" of the Jack Black quote with something like, "Black warned just last week that current economic fundamentals do not support sustainable growth, and that a recession could arrive before the end of the year."

Now let's look at which pictures actually go on the screen.

> On average, you probably want to use no more than seven or eight slides—not including the logo/name "bookend" slides we talked about a minute ago for top and bottom.

I'm talking here about the cream in the Oreo.

If you happen to be a CEO, you might even want to forget about slides altogether, because the higher you go in an organization, the less value you derive from visual aids (providing, as I say, that you know the rules of the game). With *rare* exceptions, leaders should *never* rely on slide shows. They should leave the PowerPoint to subordinates and rely exclusively on the stand-alone horsepower of the POWER formula, unembellished with visual assists of any kind. But others in the C-suite, such as the chief investment officer, chief financial officer, chief technology officer, and chief operating officer, could probably benefit from PowerPoint—providing only that it is applied sparingly, thoughtfully, and in keeping with the guidance in this chapter.

> The more you rely on slides, the less likely you will come across as a leader.

If you plan to use visual aids, your objective should be clear: each slide must make a significant business point to support the theme (projection, change, trend, solution). Any slide that provides any kind of extraneous information or data, such as columns of numbers that tell us nothing, does not make the cut. Slides that have no business in the presentation should all wind up in the hard copy or document.

It is true that a picture can be worth a thousand words. But a simple picture that says a lot is worth a thousand times more than a complicated picture that winds up adding very little and saying next to nothing.

Here are some PowerPoint guidelines:

Keep it simple—just one point per slide. Don't make the common error of thinking that if you pack a slide with numerical data, multiple graphics, and bullets you are being economical and efficient and doing your audience a favor.

The more dense the slide, the more incomprehensible it becomes (not to mention the fact that the numbers and letters keep getting smaller the more you try to fit in). Actually, you are making the processing of information a lot harder than it has to be, because what does it profit us to use fewer slides if the audience doesn't get it?

The more information you pile on, the larger the distraction and the more likely your audience will be out of sync with you. And the more you pile on, the bigger the chance for confusion and questions that may lead to frustration.

The more information you give, the more likely you are to drift away from your theme and into the weeds, and the more likely you are to go off on tangents and wind up telling your audience more—*a lot more*—than they want or need to know.

In most cases, you can easily break down even the most complex slide into several separate images.

Exception to the keep-it-simple rule: Sometimes design engineers, scientists, teachers, or technicians by necessity have to show complex schematics—design of a jet engine or complicated electrical blue-print, for example. That's fine. In this case, the schematic can remain on the screen as long as it takes to reveal the design or explain the problem or solution.

A very busy slide crammed with data can also be a good thing:

♦ If you deliberately want to obfuscate rather than clarify (for example, if the news is bad and you feel obliged not to tell all)

♦ If you want to impress your audience with the complexity of the issue, enormity of the available information, or outright sil-liness of a government or bureaucratic process

♦ If you want to make the point that your recommendations and conclusions derive from deep and thorough research. You don't expect your audience to study every line or seek out every number. You are just trying to make a valid point. In that case, clutter can be an asset. You can make it even easier by throw-ing in a line such as, "All these data and endless numbers are telling us just one thing . . ."

Use only graphics, schematics, tables, illustrations, or photos. Col-ors are better than black and white. What I would call primary colors such as blue, green, red, yellow orange, green, black, and purple (used sparingly) are generally better than pastels. White or yellow words and numbers on a royal blue or black backdrop are nice. Black print on white background is not as effective. A blue or black backdrop is preferable to a white backdrop because white illu-mination on the wall generates glare. Keep your colors *consistent throughout*: green, say, for your company, yellow for your nearest competitor, and orange for the industry norm.

Make every slide count. To know which slides, if any, you should use, ask yourself: Does this picture help make my case or support my thesis? For example, does it reflect a new situation, a prevailing condition, or plausible projection? Does it support the theme?

Stick to the basics. Trend lines, bar charts, step charts, cluster schematics, and pie charts will always serve you well. You can find them all in various designs in PowerPoint. Animated graphics can be fun to design and fun to watch, but if they are too dazzling, they can come at the expense of what you are trying to say. Like pound cake, they should be enjoyed in small bites.

One image, one concept. You may want to show, for example, a graphic contrasting two years in which your market share went up. The conventional way to do that is to show two pie charts side by side. This works (both on a screen and in decks), but on the screen it is more effective to show first the one year; then the other. Advantages of isolating the two include:

- The image is now at least twice as large on the screen, making it easier to read and grasp at a glance.
- The concept stands alone, so we can focus on one year at a time. This gives us a moment to study the wedges in the pie and how they relate to the big picture.
- When the second image comes up, we can now fully appreciate the striking difference between the two.

Make sure the size of your graphic (e.g., pie chart) reflects any change in your company's size. Say, for instance, that seven years ago your company took in 28 percent of its revenues from an international food business. Then say that today the percentage of revenues from the international food business has grown to 47 percent. But let's also say that in the meantime your company had acquired two other consumer product companies and was now three times as big as it was just seven years ago. To dramatize this change in size, your contrasting, or second image, would appear roughly three times as big as the first. So contrasting slides show not only the revenue change but also the size change.

Use graphics for good news and tables for news that may be not so good. Graphics are easier to understand than tables (which are only graphics in raw data form). The graphic is a visual interpretation of the story behind the numbers and what all that data are trying to tell us. So it only follows that if you show a graphic, you can expect people to quickly grasp the point. By contrast, tables are sets of numbers, often lots and lots of numbers, and are much harder to comprehend at a glance. *Tables can often confound. Graphics usually clarify.*

If you are not eager to dwell on a difficult issue but are obliged to touch on it, always opt for the table.

Exception to the graphics versus table question: Financial services people—analysts and others—love tables and often don't even want to hear about graphics. So in certain financial presentations (e.g., CFO reports and analyst presentations), the usual vehicle of choice may continue to be tables. This, after all, is what they are accustomed to and comfortable with, all the way from high school economics classes right through business school. But an analyst or CFO talking to a general audience had better be prepared to use graphics.

Eliminate clutter. Take out the usual bullets, text, and footnotes (unless required by regulation) that take up space on the graphics slide. Keep the original version of the slide, with all the words and bullets, for the document. Strip out numbers and dates that are not essential.

Now with your new, uncluttered version of the same slide, you can enlarge the picture until it fills the whole screen. This image in itself makes an impressive statement. Bigger impact and easier to view: this has a positive psychological effect. *Replace the words that are no longer on the slide with your own commentary.* In other words, talk about what your audience would have otherwise had to read.

Highlight important numbers, columns, sections, or whatever you want people to see. You can use different colors, a larger size font, or both. Green is for good news (profits and upswings). Red is for bad news, losses, or downswings.

Remove the "north" and "east" sides of a bordered slide to enlarge the graphic and focus attention on the concept. The more radical among us would remove the "south" and "west" borders, as well.

Be a good guide. After your roll-in, and after the next slide appears on the screen, tell your audience what they should be looking at. As in, "Take a look at the number at the bottom of the first column. That's the number we are going to have to beat," or "The cluster of little red triangles in the upper right corner of the screen tells us that the domestic housing market is about to tank."

Even if your slide has color guidance indicators, your audience may not be able to decipher them. So be sure to explain the not so obvious. As in, "Here the orange line represents the industry average . . . the yellow line is our closest competitors . . . and we are the green line, which as you can see, is trending up steeply as of the third quarter of last year . . ."

Add a blank slide. Throw in a blank slide (royal blue or black) whenever you have to spend a little time talking about something that has nothing to do with your last slide. A couple of minutes exploring a matter that does not sync or complement what is on the screen is obviously not helpful. When you have covered what you wanted to say, simply introduce your next graphic or chart with a roll-in, and the PowerPoint marches on.

Now if we put some of these practices to work, we might start with something like this fairly routine and nondescript operations statement:

	2010	2011	2012	2013	2014
			Year Ended December 31,		
			(In Thousands, Except Per Share Data)		
Statement of operations data					
New revenues					
Widget	$3,016	$5,834	$9,999	$12,720	$14,821
Knickknack	4	1,302	1,836	2,960	5,815
Other	—	150	112	676	664
Total net revenues	3,020	7,286	11,947	16,356	20,800
Gross profit	1,734	4,664	7,864	10,288	1,351
Expenses					
Selling	1,933	2,618	3,364	4,008	4,958
Marketing	151	87	246	1,035	1,433
Research and development	657	493	966	1,667	1,899
General and administrative	1,535	1,331	2,129	2,518	3,171
Total expenses	4,276	4,529	6,705	9,228	11,461
Income (loss) before					
international operating expenses, net	(2,542)	135	1,159	1,060	1,890
International operating expenses, net (1)	—	181	460	464	943
Net interest income (expense)	(114)	57	57	(12)	85
Provision for income taxes (2)	—	—	6	30	24
Net income (loss)	$(2,656)	$11	$750	$554	$1,008
Net income (loss) per share	$(1.24)	$—	$.20	$.14	$.25
Weighted average shares outstanding	2,148	3,514	3,707	3,906	4,095

This chart might suffice for an accountant or financial manager who is used to working almost exclusively with tables. But for a nonfinancial audience interested only in total net revenues, we may want to redesign a portion of the table to look more like this:

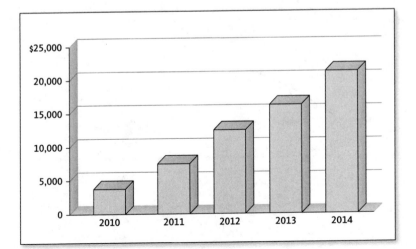

Remove all borders and a few numbers and you get this:

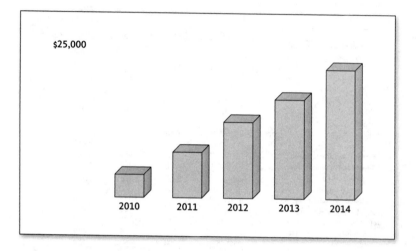

Break down to a simple line chart and you get this:

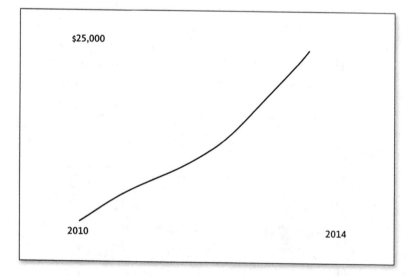

Beef up the line chart so everyone can see it—even fifty rows back:

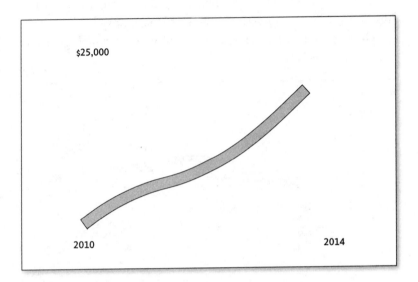

Now throw everything but the graphic away, and you finally wind up with this:

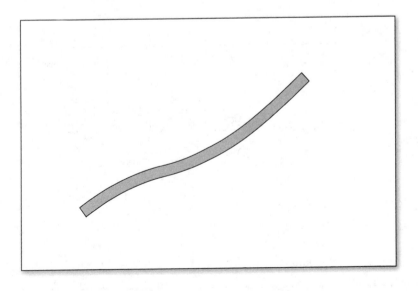

Few people ever actually dare go this far, for fear of looking jarringly different from their peers. But those who have tried, at least in my experience, have been applauded, not condemned, for the freshness, clarity, and novelty of their unique approach.

Going back to the statement-of-operations slide, you might show net income this way:

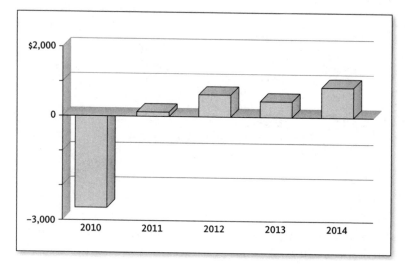

Or like this:

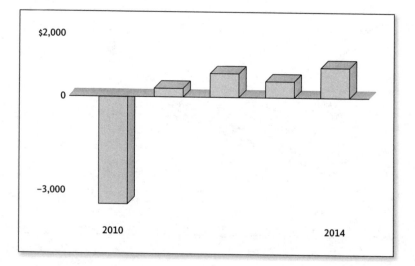

Or this:

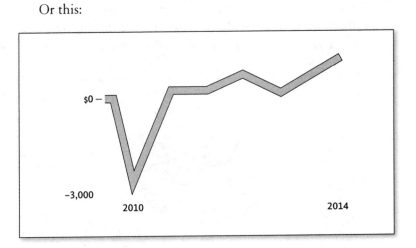

A change in market share is usually depicted in this way:

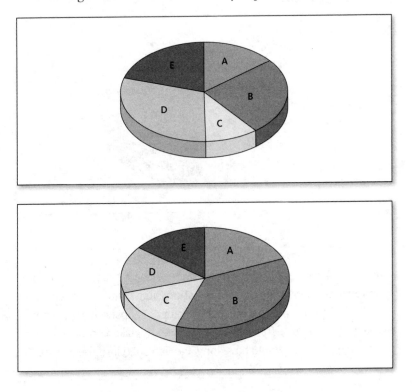

But a true reflection of market share when you measure that share in a larger market should be depicted in contrasting pie charts where the larger market—a larger pie—shows a visible contrast:

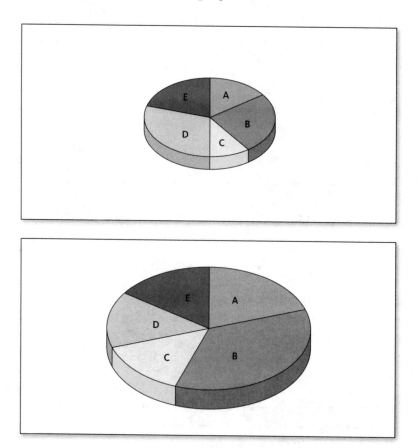

In each case, simplicity and focus seem to leap out at us. The information is condensed into the starkest possible terms and then catapulted into our minds as images that act as snapshots of concept. Weeks later we may still remember the nearly naked graph, whereas a complex table would have long ago vanished into the vapors.

If the news is good, or at least encouraging, try using fat arrows instead of skinny trend lines to emphasize growth, higher revenues, increased profits, improved market share, or what have you. Then instead of this:

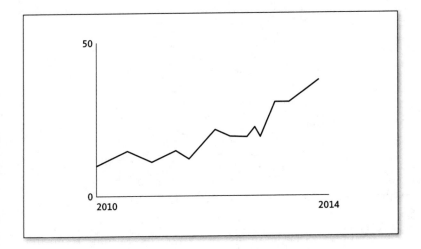

you could show something like this:

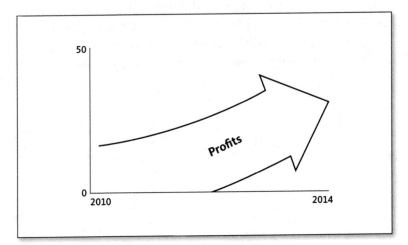

(**Caution:** Don't even think of using this kind of sweeping trend design if your audience expects real attention to every detail.)

Or even this:

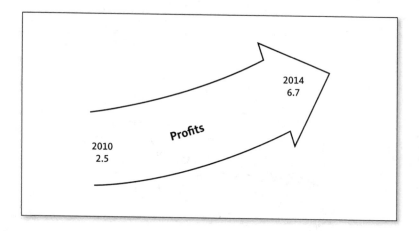

No one will fault you for using the conventional trend-line approach, and I do not have strong feelings on the matter. But arrows—especially in presentations involving larger audiences—bring *good* responses. That in itself might be reason enough to try them. But you should seek the advice and talents of a good graphics designer to figure out when it is appropriate to use arrows and how exactly to deploy them to punctuate your business message.

17

HOW TO MAKE A
POWERFUL DECK
PRESENTATION
Going by the Book

Like PowerPoint, presentation decks (sometimes also referred to as "books") have evolved into a pervasive crutch with the potential to do more harm than good, as in the following example:

A managing director of a Wall Street firm watched in horror as a presentation that could have been a piece of cake crumbled to pieces in the hands of a brilliant new hire fresh out of Harvard Business School. At stake were fees of some $30 million. The investment bankers were in the final round of a hard-fought "bake-off" to determine which firm would handle a large merger and acquisition. Another investment bank was still in the running, so while hopes were high, the outcome was still anything but certain.

The managing director led the presentation. Everything was going smoothly. In a moment, he would ask this incredibly bright young man with superior math and analytical skills to explain a particular portion of the pitch that needed technical clarification.

They had discussed the details in advance. Several minutes into the spiel, the managing director said, "I've brought Andrew with me today to elaborate on that part of the transaction," and signaled his associate to begin.

Andrew's response was perplexing. He pulled his chair back from the conference table, put his presentation deck in his lap, buried his face in it, and began to read the written text from the word slides—verbatim. His eyes never came out of his lap.

Hardly able to believe his eyes, the managing director frantically tried to make discreet hand gestures indicating that Andrew should come back to the table. Andrew misunderstood the signal to mean he was supposed to go faster. So he began to speak almost as fast as he could read.

Meanwhile, the clients, seated on the other side of the table, could only marvel at this bizarre act. By the time the managing director finally interrupted his prodigy and took back the presentation, it was too late. In the end, the business—and the $30 million that went with it—wound up in the hands of the competing investment bank.

Clearly what we had here was a *failure* to communicate. As so often happens, almost everything that could go wrong did go wrong. The deal went south. Instead of signing on, the potential partner or clients walked away feeling they may have dodged a bullet.

Aside from the obvious fact that it was a bad call to bring the kid in at a critical point in the selling process and the clear perception that there was apparently little or no coordination between the managing director and his junior associate—and certainly no planning or rehearsal for the meeting—the presence of a wordy deck at this inopportune moment did not help. Part of the lesson here is that presentation decks can be a bane and a curse—and often do *more harm* than good. That's why I am not fond of them. Few people are. Yet most people rely on them. So as in the case of all visuals, we have to make sure they work for us, never against us.

THE WAFER AND ___
THE WHOPPER

In an ideal world we would abandon the use of presentation decks altogether (except as documents of record) and happily trust our futures and fortunes to the POWER formula. Many accomplished business leaders have done just that.

For all the rest who may not have a choice, the experience, or expertise, or for whatever reason feel that they must depend on decks to see them through, there is a powerful way to use presentation decks to produce consistently good results. The rules are simple. They involve only minor changes that can make a big difference.

Here are the elements that will set you apart and help win whatever you need:

♦ *Prepare a presentation deck different from the document you leave behind.* We'll call the actual deck used in the pitch the "Wafer," because it is thin. We'll call the document left behind (or available in digital form) the "Whopper" because it is loaded with fat and weighted down with *all* the data—most of which you do not need in the pitch.

♦ *Keep the book closed in the beginning of the meeting and again at the end* (you may not even have to open it at all). This may remind you of the Oreo.

♦ *Use **no** word slides.* (They end up in the document, which you keep to yourself as a reference only, or to help answer questions. If the client insists on a Whopper copy, let the client have it afterward or arrange to have it sent digitally.)

♦ *Stick to the same design and color guidelines for visual aids outlined in the previous chapter.*

♦ *Whenever possible, hand the decks out **after** the presentation, not before.* This implies the pitch occurs without a book, which can sometimes be a very good thing. Sometimes the client will insist on the deck at the table, which we will deal with later.

♦ *Unleash the POWER formula.* Strong start. One theme. Examples to back up the theme. Ordinary language. Strong ending.

A typical deck presentation may go something like this:

Businesspeople gather in a conference room and take their seats, usually on opposite sides of the table. The presenting team makes some formal introductions all around the table. The lead player announces how much the team appreciates this opportunity to make this presentation. Next he opens the presentation deck, very likely to the agenda page, and tells everybody to do the same. Then he reads or paraphrases the agenda line for line.

Finally, the presentation begins—but it is just one word slide after another. The lead player is reading from his own deck, so everyone in the room is following his lead—and now everybody is reading and nobody is paying attention to what the lead player is saying. Worse, soon everybody is out of sync because they can read faster than he can talk. People are flipping through pages. This is troubling—but it's just the beginning. Very soon it is clear that there is no theme, just information that may not be relevant to the business needs of the client. Another presenter is formally introduced. She reads more word slides. It only gets worse. The scenario can take many unfortunate turns from here (e.g., drag on for forty-five agonizing minutes) but will always wind up in the same black hole: time wasted and another opportunity lost.

On any given day, you can see variations of this sorry scene replayed in thousands of conference rooms across the United States and around the world. It is a tale of mediocrity made manifest—a needless squandering of potential—and yet still the current standard of practice for millions of unwitting businesspeople who are no doubt left scratching their heads and wondering why they did not get the contract.

So how do we right this wrong? Here's a different scenario:

Businesspeople gather in a conference room. The presenting team makes a point of getting the introductions out of the way before everyone is seated; this keeps formalities at a minimum and gets things off to a faster start. If the hosts want to chitchat a little after sitting down (e.g., maybe talk about the weather or politics), that's fine. Otherwise the presenting lead should look for the first opportunity to begin. This could come as a sudden silence or a signal such as, "So, Mary, what have you got?"

For the sake of illustration, let's assume that in this particular case the hosts have requested that the deck be made available in advance or insisted that it be physically on the table for the meeting.

Now for the lead to control the meeting, the deck must not yet be opened. If someone across the table happens to be peeking inside and sneaking a look ahead, the lead immediately puts an end to that with something like: "Before we get into the books there is something I think you need to know first" or "Before we look at the books, let me first give you the big picture."

If the lead feels secure, is comfortable with the POWER formula, and is completely confident with her story, she may choose a more radical approach. For example, if the meeting is small (just a couple of people), she might dismiss the books altogether with something like: "We have a whole presentation here in this deck, but instead of dwelling on the book, I think I'd just like to give you a quick overview of how we see the situation and how I think we might be able to help."

If you have the time, make two presentations: the Wafer that shows only visuals and graphics, and the Whopper that documents everything else, such as word slides and dense tables of support and backup data.

The rest is straight out of the POWER playbook: No opening amenities. No agenda. No further mention of a presentation. (We want this to feel and sound like a *conversation*, which sets the right mood, brings us closer to our hosts, and immediately improves our chances of success.) Instead of opening amenities and all the usual palaver, the lead is fast off the mark with a strong start (Chapter 8). That's why she insists the book remain closed.

If her gut tells her that this crowd is a little prickly, proud, insecure, or defensive, or if the other party's agenda is not entirely clear, she may want to go with a different tack and put the ball in the other court, as in: "Rather than jump into the decks, let me first ask—how do you think we can be of service?"

If possible, do not hand out any materials until you are finished talking. If you must hand them out, hold them until the first graphic. Otherwise, just follow the protocols in this chapter.

If the book plays any role in this pitch, it will come only after the lead has galvanized the minds in the room with a commanding opening. And as mentioned in an earlier chapter, she will make it her business to make sure the whole theme, the entire story, is already on the table before the book is opened—even though her hosts may not realize it.

After a strong opening that has everybody in the room wide awake and wanting to hear more, the lead may choose to turn to the deck (the proof and the cream filling in the Oreo). Now her role shifts to that of lawyer. The case has been presented, and it is time to prove it. So she will summon a roll-in, such as, "So what does that look like? Take a look at page one." Then she leads the room by physically opening the book.

If for any reason there was no time to prepare a Wafer, she will open the Whopper to the exact page she needs to support her point. She might say, for example: "You can see how we expect the upturn to rebalance the market with a return to normal pricing on page thirty-eight." After that, she will continue to roll in to perhaps half a dozen pages scattered throughout the Whopper that help seal the deal.

Now comes the critical moment when she turns a portion of the pitch over to a partner or subordinate. That person may be charged with, say, fleshing out the financials. But instead of, "Now I would like to turn the presentation over to . . . ," she simply stops talking.

Seamlessly, the next speaker jumps right in. This little bit of stagecraft is important because it gives the hosts the perception that the lead and her associates really are a team. They seem to think as one mind and speak as one voice.

"The next step is to support that business model [that Mary's been talking about] with a strong balance sheet and cash flow," the CFO suddenly chimes in, and now all eyes are on him. But Mary, for her part, stays attentive. She does not look down nor appear to be distracted. She continues to make eye contact around the table and glances often at her CFO. He may run with the ball for a few minutes, as long as it takes to position the financials along the lines of Mary's theme so that everything is lined up and going in the same direction. Every graph and chart makes the story ever stronger, and the theme—let's say the game-changing importance of a particular global strategy—resonates in the evidence he presents.

When he winds up his portion, he throws in a line that holds to the theme and gives him a robust exit, as in, "So as you can see, we are putting every penny, every dime to work to secure a market foothold in India and China by the end of the year." Then he makes a point of closing the book. Mary does too.

Not missing a beat, Mary now picks it up for a drive to the finish with something like, "So it all comes down to this . . ." She delivers a strong ending, and depending on whether she senses the energy in the room is right, she might toss out a final line: "What do you think?"

The response could be that they need time to discuss the proposal among themselves or it might lead to a fertile Q&A period and the possibility of closing the deal right then and there.

I can tell you from experience that this approach can eclipse the competition and make the difference between failure and success.

A FINAL WORD ON
—— POWERPOINT AND ——
PRESENTATION DECKS

Using this new methodology we've been talking about does not always make sense. The exception to the rule is when companies send out rookies and recent hires to give new business and sales presentations. These are people who do not have a depth of knowledge about their products or companies, nor do they have a lot of speaking experience. If the meeting is important, they have no business being out there in the first place. So it is probably a good idea to load them up with heavy visual aid support that can provide some quality control and consistency of presentation and allow them to stay a little more in the background, where they belong. In a special case like this, many of the old rules could apply. (Of course, as I have said, the *real* answer to this question is that companies should **never** send very junior people to give any kind of presentation—unless those people have been thoroughly, correctly trained and prepared.)

By contrast, the further up one goes within organizations, *the less desirable* it becomes to rely too heavily on visual aids until you arrive ultimately at the office of the chairman, who should **never** use them.

—— FLIP CHARTS ——

Flip charts are most useful in highly interactive meetings, such as "ideation" sessions where things are moving fast, creativity is flowing, and ideas are popping up one after another—because they capture ideas before they vanish.

But if you choose to use flip charts as conventional visual aids, with graphs, schematics, tables, data, and pictures, kind of like a low-tech PowerPoint presentation, then treat them as you would a PowerPoint, with the same guidelines you read in Chapter 16. In other words, forget word slides and show information only *after* you have explained what the audience is about to see.

To control the audience's "eye," you would have to *leave every other page blank*. In this way, the conversation comes right back to you after the flip chart page has served its purpose. That's what you want. You want the presentation to gravitate back to you as soon as possible.

A few easy tips to remember with flip charts:

- Prepare your flip charts in advance, if possible.
- Use heavy, wide-tip markers that make a bold line clearly legible from thirty feet away.
- Leave every other page blank.
- Make sure all letters and numbers are at least two inches tall. Leave a separation of at least three inches between lines.
- Use color—but use it consistently to represent class or category throughout your presentation as you would with PowerPoint.
- Try to write in block capital letters only (assuming that you feel you must use words). Block letters are consistent in shape, larger than lowercase lettering, and if not too crowded together, easiest to read on a flip chart.
- Try to write while facing the audience. For some people, this is too difficult. For these people, I would suggest (1) keep writing to a minimum—or prepare your flip charts in advance, and (2) write clearly and quickly when you do have to turn your back to the audience.

—— CONFERENCE ROOM ——
WALL PRESENTATIONS

The rule here is very simple. If you choose not to use a whiteboard and intend to hang your presentation (flip chart paper) on the perimeter walls of a conference room in a more interactive and physical "drill down" or "workout" format, be certain you reveal only one section at a time as you proceed around the room. This way you will be able to control your audience's attention much better than if they were constantly surrounded on all sides by detailed information. You may need an assistant to cover up the old panels as you move into the new ones. As with PowerPoint and presentation decks, try to tell the story of what's on the next panel before you actually show the panel.

18

WRITE LIKE YOU SPEAK
Ten Important Rules to Live By

S PEAKING FROM A text is *rarely* a good idea (with the notable exceptions of testimony, legally sensitive issues, time restrictions, little preparation time, lack of experience, etc.) and the rest of the time is not a good idea *at all*. But if you must do a prepared text, then it only makes sense that the words in your text reflect the way you naturally talk. If they are written in the style of an academic tome or policy memorandum (i.e., subjunctive clauses, long sentences, clumsy language, and all the rest), then you will struggle against almost insurmountable odds.

So you don't want to wrestle with a jellyfish. You will drown trying.

What you *do* want is something that allows you to sound like yourself, perhaps even *be* yourself. The closest any of us can ever get to sounding like ourselves with a prepared text is to make sure the writing is simple. That's the *secret* behind every great speech. Every great speechwriter knows that the most direct way to the audience's hearts and minds is to speak directly.

The simply written speech makes it possible for *any* speaker to invest style and personality into the words and then into the audience.

Most people don't understand the *difference* between writing for the ear and writing for the eye. Ideally, there is no difference. But for the majority of people there will always be a big difference. A surprising number of businesspeople write their own speeches. But how they write those speeches makes it virtually impossible for them to look or sound the way they naturally talk. In other words, they defeat themselves even before they begin. Unwittingly, they create a vehicle without wheels. That's because the way we speak is often *not* the way we write.

The solution is simple: *Write the way you speak.* To help you write the way you speak, I have assembled a few easy writing rules:

1. Keep your sentences short. If you have a sentence with a number of subordinate clauses, *break it down* into bite-sized pieces. Or break it up with three dots (. . .) placed strategically throughout the long sentence in several places. Or simply translate the long sentence into a short one. For example:

> Too-long sentence: *It is necessary to reexamine our intentions, and the attendant responsibilities that we understand lie ahead, in order that we may have a more disciplined approach to the challenges presented by the new tax legislation, which is presently, in any event, expected to reveal a number of surprises for our members, who can take some comfort in the fact that the tax laws, as we have experienced them in the last five years, have been generally favorable for people in an income bracket exceeding $100,000.*

> Revised: *The tax laws will change, and those changes will have a material effect on each of us.*

2. Choose the active voice. Wherever possible, avoid the passive voice. The passive voice is the voice of the bureaucrat. (Of course, if you want deliberately to obfuscate, then by all means use the passive voice.) The passive voice takes the "actor"—you—out of the action, but the active voice puts the actor back in. Examples:

PASSIVE VOICE: *It is imperative that the defense establishment be refurbished in order that the military operation can be prosecuted.*

REVISED: *Give us the tools and we will finish the job. (Winston Churchill in a letter to President Roosevelt)*

PASSIVE VOICE: *It is obligatory that all illumination be extinguished before the premises are vacated. (government bureaucrat)*

REVISED: *Turn off the lights when you leave. (FDR telling government bureaucrat how to translate the preceding sentence)*

3. Pick short, conversational words. Avoid *archaic* language that still lingers in the lexicon but is fast on its way out. We are still probably years ahead of ourselves on this one, but I still prefer to err on the side of economy.

Here are some examples:

OLD: Notwithstanding *our commitment to keep out of the dispute, we should still try to do something to resolve the conflict.*

REVISED: *In spite of our commitment to keep out of the dispute, we should still try to do something to resolve the conflict.*

OLD: Inasmuch *as we are all in this together, we should probably try to cooperate rather than argue.*

REVISED: *Since we are all in this together, we should probably try to cooperate rather than argue.*

OLD: Therefore, *we should take it upon ourselves to provide the necessary leadership.*

REVISED: *So we should take it upon ourselves to provide the necessary leadership.*

OLD: Moreover, *we have not yet heard a believable argument from the other side.*

REVISED: *What's more, we have not yet heard a believable argument from the other side.*

OLD: However, *we were unable to reserve a seat for the performance.*

REVISED: *But we were unable to reserve a seat for the performance. (Some people cling to the notion that it is not OK to start a sentence with but. This argument was more credible thirty years ago than it is today. I take the position that the language is changing fast and that starting with but today is not only permissible but actually desirable—because it is more conversational, whether in writing or speaking.)*

OLD: Furthermore, *our budget will not allow us to take on an extra project this year.*

REVISED: *Not only that, but our budget will not allow us to take on an extra project this year.*

As a rule, speakers should opt for the revised versions and leave the "dinosaur" words to the lawyers and bureaucrats who are so loathe to give them up. (Which is not to say that if you happen to be a lawyer or bureaucrat you can't also be an effective speaker. But if all lawyers and bureaucrats spoke the way many of them write, we would need professional translators in every courthouse and state capitol.)

4. Avoid buzzwords. Corporate speeches and presentations are often swarming with "bumblebees":

BUZZWORD: *This solution is one that we believe to be viable.*

REVISED: *We think this solution will work.*

BUZZWORD: *It is necessary that we* interface *with our research and development employees.*

REVISED: *We've got to sit down and talk with our R&D people.*

BUZZWORD: *Therefore, we must* maintain a dialogue.

REVISED: *So let's keep talking.*

BUZZWORD: *The results of our sales survey will* impact *the bottom line.*

REVISED: *The results of our sales survey will have an impact on the bottom line. (It is still preferable to use* impact *as a noun.)*

BUZZWORD: *We must garner our* resources *to compete in the marketplace.*

REVISED: *To compete, we've got to spend more money on R&D and on our own people.*

BUZZWORD: *With work, we can expect to achieve* superior synergy.

REVISED: *We expect a good fit.*

BUZZWORD: *One of our goals is to enter into a policy of* empowerment *with our human resources.*

REVISED: *We are going to let our own people make their own decisions and be accountable for the results.*

Not everyone will fault you for sounding like a bumblebee—mainly because many others in the organization have probably got the buzz, too. But you can distinguish yourself and become a more believable speaker (while still remaining a team player) simply by shooing the bumblebee out of your language.

5. Be specific. Don't rely on indefinite reference pronouns—the *he's, she's, they's, them's, it's, one's,* and *we's* that clutter our everyday conversation. Repetition in prose is a vice that should be avoided. But repetition in rhetoric is a device that should be encouraged. Examples:

> Pronouns: We *told* them *that* he *would take* one *to* him, *but she said* they *gave* it *to* him, *before* he *had a chance to read* it.

> Specific: *Bob and I told the management committee that Dan would take a copy of the document to Tom, but Alice said the board gave the proposal to us before Dan had even read the proposal.*

This is an extreme example, perhaps, but it illustrates that important pronouns can easily get lost. It's not uncommon, for example, to be talking about several *him*'s at once in the same sentence. Great care should be taken that people always understand exactly whom you are talking about at all times. I have heard reports of more than one deal going sour because the listeners misunderstood the pronoun. Who is *he*? What exactly is *it*?

If you are reading a newspaper article, or an e-zine or blog on your desktop, you can follow the reference pronoun because you need only track back to the beginning of the sentence to find out who the *he* is referring to. But when someone is talking, you have no way of checking the reference—unless you interrupt that person and ask, for example, "Which *he* are you talking about?" Common courtesy would restrain most people from asking that kind of question, and you may not know that your listeners are already lost.

I remember once when I sat in on one of my daughter's college classes, the professor's command of his subject profited him little in the face of a daunting barrage of self-inflicted pronouns. He was describing the similarities between Fascism and Communism, with Nazis and Blackshirts in the Fascist camp and Leninists and Marxists in the Communist camp—a total of six separate entities. He paced around the stage talking excitedly about "it," "that," "one," "them," and "they." Individuals melted into "him" and "he." It soon became impossible to figure out who was who and what was what. In the end, after an hour and a quarter and in spite of his enthusiastic delivery, the students left the room not much more enlightened than when they walked in. That's a waste of talent and time, and it's one case when you can blame a lack of knowledge—not of subject but of the correct use of pronouns.

So repeat the name again and again when you're speaking. Instead of, "We told them that that was one that she said he would give to me," say, "Our firm told the opposing lawyers that this case was the case that Bob's secretary said the boss would give to me." Still convoluted, but it's a lot clearer than an omelet of indefinite reference pronouns.

6. Avoid sweeping generalities. Sweeping generalities, like sheepdogs, tend to hide more than they reveal. For example:

> GENERALITY: *Now is the time that this nation should begin thinking seriously again about tapping* alternative energy sources.

> REVISED: *Now is the time to start thinking seriously again about tidal and wind power and solar and nuclear energy.*

> GENERALITY: *Now more than ever this country must depend on her* learning institutions *to produce an educated and productive population for the future.*

> REVISED: *Now more than ever we must depend on our universities, public and private schools, vocational centers, community colleges, hospitals, and corporate training centers to produce an educated and productive population for the future.*

The "sheepdog" races in one ear and right out the other.

The more "snapshots"—brief concrete images—that you give people, the more likely they are to remember what you said.

7. Don't use confusing words. Some words send out signals that often can be misleading and fuzzy. Examples:

> Fuzzy: *I would like to* cite *that* site *as just one more example of how we have lost* sight *of our environmental mandate.*

> Clear: *That location is just one more example of how we have lost sight of our environmental mandate.*

> Fuzzy: *The city building codes require that we* raze *[sounds like* raise*] all buildings that are beyond repair.*

> Clear: *The city building codes require that we tear down all buildings that are beyond repair.*

> Fuzzy: *I found all the hectic activity leading up to the wedding to be* enervating *[sounds like* energize, *but actually means "draining"].*

> Clear: *I found all the hectic activity leading up to the wedding to be exhausting.*

> Fuzzy: *When we hurt the tourist industry, we are in effect cutting off our* air line *[means "oxygen hose," but sounds like Jet Blue].*

> Clear: *When we hurt the tourist industry, we are in effect cutting off our lifeline.*

In the age of AIDS awareness, *conundrum* begins to sound a lot like *condom*. Difficult-to-pronounce words like *conundrum, covetousness,* or *problematic* probably ought to be left out (Jerry Ford couldn't pronounce *nuclear,* so instead he had to say *atomic*).

Sometimes words can be used deliberately, for whatever reason, to send a hidden or tongue-in-cheek message. In his book *The Lexicon of Intentionally Ambiguous Recommendations,* Lehigh University economist Robert Thornton came up with devilishly clever ways to write recommendations for lousy job candidates. For example:

For a candidate with "interpersonal" problems, he suggests: *"I am pleased to say this person is a former colleague of mine."*

For the lazy worker: *"In my opinion, you will be very fortunate to get this person to work for you."*

For the criminal: *"He's a man of many convictions,"* and *"I'm sorry we let him get away."*

For the untrustworthy job seeker: *"Her true ability is deceiving."*

And for the inept worker: *"I most enthusiastically recommend this person with no qualifications whatsoever."*

Those little beauties are all on purpose, of course, and illustrate the curious ambiguity of the language. But some poor souls put their feet in their mouths and don't even know it. In the *Wall Street Journal*, personnel expert Robert Half noted these clunkers that landed on his desk in star-crossed résumés:

I am a rabid typist.
Thank you for your consideration. Hope to hear from you shorty.
Here are my qualifications for you to overlook . . .

8. Skip the puffed-up, self-serving "peacock" language, couched in superlatives, that strains credulity. I'm talking about the kind of preening talk ("the greatest," "the finest," "the most exemplary") that often finds its way into the canned spiel of elected officials.

Peacock language is: ". . . and I say to you, my fellow Americans, that the time has come for a new day for America, a day of renewed hope and the conviction to meet the challenges of the future." The same old speech—we've all heard it a thousand times.

The same message, couched in more believable language, is: "The worst is now probably behind us. The future won't be easy—

no question. But working together I see no reason why we can't accomplish whatever we make up our minds to accomplish." By toning down the rhetoric we have recast a message of hope into language and terms that people can identify with.

You know you're hearing peacock language when someone says: "It's not the money—it's the principle!" (You know that person already has got a hand in your pocket.) Or "To be honest with you . . ." (What has that person been the rest of the time, dishonest?). Or when the CEO reminisces about "my best years" spent on the factory floor. Or when the speechwriter has the CEO say: "Profits are secondary! What we're really interested in is people." Or the limousine liberal who flies in from his summer house in the Hamptons to tell an audience: "I can't sleep at night thinking about the plight of blacks in America."

> To be credible, you also must accept the notion that one simple unembellished truth in the right place can carry more weight than a whole marching band of half-truths, euphemisms, unrealistic projections, and promises you know you can never keep. By contrast, just one phony line can drag down the integrity of all the honest lines in the rest of the speech.

We've gotten so used to superlatives, exaggerations, and misrepresentations—especially from political people—that it *almost seems natural* to stretch the truth. For example, speechwriters often stray from the believable by having principals say things like: "This is the greatest experience of my life," when, of course, it is not. *One of the greatest*, maybe; that is unarguable. But the *greatest* strains credibility and tends to taint the rest of what the speaker has to say.

Sometimes exaggerated writing begins to sound like the equivalent of elevator music. We know it's there, but it's so bland we hardly notice it: "The next twenty years will be a time of great economic challenge and opportunity for this nation. If we meet the challenge in a forthright and courageous way, we can ascend to even higher levels of prosperity; if we do not, we will slip into a steady decline to economic mediocrity." A better version is: "The next twenty years are critical. In fact, they remind me of the Chinese word for *crisis*. The Chinese use two picture characters to denote the word *crisis*. The picture word for *danger* is placed next to the picture word for *opportunity*. . . . Well, the twenty-first century can be a dangerous time of declining productivity—or a decade of opportunity with new markets and expanded growth."

Résumé writers, too, are legendary in their ability to embellish. The résumé writer will say, "spearheaded marketing, advertising, and new product development." In fact, the writer may have been just one of many marketing people assigned to three or four failed new product launches.

If all speeches told the truth (Churchill: "The news from France is very bad") we would probably be more productive. And if all résumés were true, we wouldn't have recessions.

9. Avoid weak verbs. Use stronger, active verbs wherever possible. Examples:

WEAK: *Now we must* maintain our resolve.

STRONGER: *We've got to keep fighting.*

WEAK: *This year our* growth will be sustained.

STRONGER: *This year we'll keep growing.*

WEAK: *We are also going to* reduce costs.

STRONGER: *We are also going to cut costs* (cut *for moderate,* slash *for extreme).*

WEAK: *And we expect to* incur *a loss.*

STRONGER: *And we expect to lose some money.*

Weak: *In the end, we hope to evince a profit.*

Stronger: *In the end we hope to make money.*

10. Keep a tight leash on statistics. Statistics tend to proliferate like rabbits in business presentations of all kinds. Polls tell us that audiences can't remember more than one key figure at a time The ear is not a funnel into which we can pour information. *Too many facts can defeat the communication.*

Some quick tips for rabbit control (managing statistics):

◆ Pick the most important.
◆ Round them off.
◆ Dress them up.

The following are examples of rabbits and their revisions:

Rabbits: *Market share increased 3.2 percent, from 5 percent to 8.2 percent in the last quarter, compared to an increase of 4.5 percent, up to a high of 13.5 percent from a low of 9 percent in the same quarter last year. (That's too many numbers for the brain to manage—especially if the rest of the presentation is also liberally laced with statistics. Worse, the construction is clumsy.)*

Revised: *Market share was off more than 5 percent this year.*

Rabbits: *Production increased 6.3 percent from 8.1 billion bbl to 10.2 billion bbl from 2010 to 2011. (Still too much stuff.)*

Revised: *Production was up more than 6 percent—roughly two billion barrels in the last year alone. That's enough oil to heat Boston for ten years.*

We dress up the statistic to give meaning to the otherwise meaningless concept of "a barrel of oil." People can't picture two billion barrels of oil. So you make an analogy almost anyone can identify with—especially if you are talking to a nonindustry audience.

A good analogy can make all the difference. As a client of mine puts it, a good analogy can light up the room. Here's another example:

> RABBITS: *Increased productivity worldwide is projected to rise by 2 percent or 99.3 million tons per year in terms of edible grains.*

This dry little sentence is not only badly written ("in terms of . . ."—passive voice, and "edible grains"—a sheepdog) but also provokes a big "So what?" When we dress it up, we might get something like:

> REVISED: *Increased productivity worldwide will mean another 2 percent of rice, corn, and wheat a year—roughly 100 million tons. That's enough food to feed every hungry mouth in the Third World for three months.*

The food analogy provides not only dramatic perspective and dimension but also the all-important human element that makes the numbers, and the business behind them, seem to come alive.

The insurance industry is notoriously fond of statistics as we can see in the following examples:

> RABBITS: *During the past five years, property and casualty premiums have grown at a 15.6 percent average compound annual growth rate to $90.1 billion. Personal lines have grown to $38.4 billion (a 14 percent annual growth rate), and commercial lines have grown to $51.7 billion—a 16.7 percent compound annual growth rate.*

> REVISED: *During the past five years, property and casualty premiums have grown to more than $90 billion. That's enough insurance to insure every house and car in England. Put another way, if your salary had gone up at the same rate and you were earning $18,000 a year in 1979, today you'd be making $116,000 a year.*

RABBITS: *The top four firms—of which ours is second—wrote 21 percent of the business. The top eight firms wrote 32 percent, and the top twenty firms wrote 54 percent. The top fifty firms wrote 75 percent of the business.*

REVISED: *We're kind of the "Avis" of insurance. We're only second—but we try harder. The result is that we have a big share of the business. Overall in the industry, the top four firms wrote about a fifth of the business. The top eight firms wrote about a third—and the top twenty firms wrote a little more than half.*

19

THE SIX MOST COMMON
LANGUAGE MISTAKES

*As far as profits, if we would have kept the factory where it's at,
there's three things we should have done in terms of productivity
for the managers that have to run it.*

Apart from being hopelessly unwieldy, this sentence embraces
six of the most woefully abused language mistakes we hear not
only in business but in life itself. Four of the six betray the speaker
as someone with an incomplete education. The fifth—a numbing
reliance on the phrase *in terms of*—just indicates lazy talk (and lazy
writing).

Now look at this:

As far as profits are concerned, if we had *kept the factory where
it was,* we now see *three things we should have done* to boost
productivity (for the managers who have to run the factory).

You can see that remedying the biggest goofs comes down to a quick
fix. (*For the managers who have to run the factory* is unnecessary. I've

left it in only to make a point.) Anyone can easily upgrade the quality of their speaking and writing by getting rid of just a few bad habits:

1. *As far as* always requires *is* (or *are*) *concerned* or *goes* to complete the thought or phrase. It always has to be *as far as something goes* or *is concerned*—not just *as far as something*. So the sentence should read, "As far as profits go . . ." or "As for profits . . ." or just plain, "Looking at profits . . ."

2. The conditional subjunctive can never be expressed as *if I would have* or *if she would have* or *if they would have.* The correct way to follow *if* is to use *had* with the verb—"If he had" or drop *if* altogether: "Were he to have" or "Had he . . ." So our sentence should read, ". . . *if we had* . . .".

3. Just one item or person requires a singular verb; more than one requires the plural. In my opinion, this is the most common rhetorical mistake of our time. For reasons frustratingly unclear, whole generations have fallen to mismatching the verb *to be* with singular and plural nouns. My kids do it, and their kids will probably wind up doing it, too. But it's wrong, and we ought to make every effort to get at least this little thing right. No more, "There's five people waiting in the conference room." Is it so tough to say, "*There are* five people"? Our sentence should read, "*There are* three things . . .".

4. *That* is for things. *Who* is for people. Instead of, "This is the woman *that*," simply make it, "This is the woman *who*." But it is, "This is the office *that*. . . ." Our sentence should read, ". . . managers *who* . . .".

5. *In terms of* is just plain tedious. It robs us of whatever action verb or economy of scale we once might have chosen to express ourselves—before we had *in terms of* to fall back on. Instead of, "We expect to improve, in terms of profits," try, "We expect to make a profit." Instead of, "In terms of labor, we are hiring more people," just say, "We're hiring more people." Instead of, "In terms of outlook, the future is not promising," try, "We could be doing a lot better." In our sentence we seek an active verb. Instead of "in terms of productivity," we choose ". . . boost productivity."

6.   Never place an *at* after *where is*. Instead of, "Where is he *at?*" or, "He knows where it's *at,*" or "I know where the files are *at,*" how about just, "Where is he?" "He knows where it is," and "I know where the files are." So our original sentence could come down to this: "If we had stayed, we would have had to boost productivity to increase profits."

If you don't think any of this matters, think again. A junior person from company A makes a sales pitch to a senior person from company B and her staff. Company A doesn't get the business—and will never know why. The reason is that although the junior person from company A was intelligent, apparently competent, and seemingly knowledgeable, he was also to some degree *inarticulate.* The senior person from B comes away with the impression that the person from A is out of his depth, in over his head, a little lacking in sophistication, a little naive perhaps, and (if the way he talked is any indication) also short on the kind of education that people from company B would look for in a business partner or relationship.

Here are a few other bear traps you might want to avoid:

INCORRECT: *"If I was him . . ."*

CORRECT: *"If I were he . . ."* (Were *must follow* if, *and* he *must follow the verb* to be.)

INCORRECT: *"You did real good."*

CORRECT: *"You did really well."* (Good *is not an adverb, and you have to throw an* ly *on an adverb that modifies another adverb.)*

These are all small fixes that can yield big payoffs. In my experience, the more articulate the presenter, the higher the potential for business success.

It may not be entirely circumstantial that few of the business and political leaders I have known commit *any* of the six most common language mistakes.

20

HOW TO BEAT FEAR

Before you can even think about talking in public, first you must deal with the enemy within: anxiety, self-doubt, stage fright, and all the other little bugaboos that in varying degrees plague most human beings. Not everybody experiences fear of taking the floor. But for those who do, performance anxiety can be a major roadblock, and we've got to find a way around it.

The good news is that fear is not all bad. Fear is the mind's wake-up call: a way to make you more alert, responsive, and fine-tuned for action. Fear is part of human nature, altogether natural, and to be expected. But out of control, fear can overwhelm and paralyze. Utter fear is utterly debilitating, and we must avoid it. The trick is to shape fear and anxiety into a tool put to our good use.

In other words, we don't want to get rid of the butterflies entirely. As a friend of mine puts it, we just want them to *fly in formation* and that requires an attitudinal adjustment.

Of course, the best way to conquer fear is to make the same speech one hundred times. But let's assume that making the same speech over and over is not a likelihood for most of us. Outside of

pharmaceuticals, prayer, or hypnosis, the only way I know to conquer fear is to change the way we perceive public speaking. It's as
simple as turning the caveman flight-or-fight mentality of cold
sweats and rapid heartbeats into an attitude of positive anticipation
and healthy challenge.

In advance of any speaking assignment, you should mentally
prepare by reminding yourself of six key points:

1. Love the people. Picture yourself on a familiar footing with the
audience. Try to have a prevailing sense of warmth and goodwill
toward the people who have come to hear you speak. Imagine yourself in the barroom we've been talking about—or in your own living
room or dining room, enthusiastically letting old friends in on an
exciting new piece of information. The truth is that most people
don't care about how much you know—until they know how much
you care. You will be surprised how this single altered perception in
itself goes a long way toward defusing your anxieties—and giving
you more "energy" than you thought you had.

2. Serve the people. Remember that you have come in *service* to these
people in the audience. You have come to serve *them*, not yourself.
They have every reason to expect something of value from you (otherwise, why show up in the first place?), and you have a responsibility to give them value. The way to deliver value is to be *more concerned
about the audience than you are about yourself.* Concentrate on the
message, not on the messenger. Focus on what you are saying, and
you won't have to worry about how you are doing. The measure of
how you are doing is proportionate to your commitment to what you
are saying.

3. You're the guru. Remind yourself that you know as much or more
about your subject than anyone in the room. This should give you
the necessary confidence to forge ahead and do well.

4. Have fun. If you have read this book and you are a player, you will. But if you still have a problem, at least tell yourself that you're having a good time. Sounds laughable, but it can help. Look at your speaking assignment as you would any other fun challenge in life—a tennis or golf game, for example. Then mentally put yourself right back in that bar with your friends.

5. Pump yourself up. Remind yourself of times in the past when you had to speak. You may not have always been perfect. But you survived. Perhaps it went very well, in which case you can congratulate yourself on a job well done and recall what it was like, how it went, what you did right, and how you felt afterward.

6. In your mind, picture yourself talking to *just one person*. If it helps, pick out one person in the audience and speak directly to him or her.

These mental games may not eliminate all your butterflies, but they should help change anxiety into a sense of excitement and challenge, which is the same frame of mind that champion athletes cultivate to win in sports.

With the architecture we've been talking about, and the foundation, and now the confidence to command the room, you are almost ready.

21

KEEP THE
MOMENTUM GOING

MARTIN LUTHER KING Jr.'s famous "I have a dream" speech way back in 1963 was a tipping point in American race relations. In less than twenty minutes, he set the stage for the civil rights movement for the next fifty years and inspired generations of Americans, black and white, to work together to try to make the issue of color a thing of the past.

This was an especially daunting challenge at a time when segregation was still alive and well, and the notion of racial equality was still, in many parts of the country, almost unthinkable.

Martin Luther King Jr. succeeded that day not just because he was a gifted orator with a special talent for impassioned rhetorical theater, and not just because he understood the needs of his audience and the power of language to change the world. He succeeded because he understood momentum.

When energy hits critical mass and becomes unstoppable, you've got momentum. And few people—before or since—have known how to harness momentum like Martin Luther King Jr.

If you go on YouTube and watch the speech, you will note that it has a rhythm that seems to gain speed, heat, and tempo. As he starts to come into the stretch, in the latter third of the address, he begins to pull out the rhetorical stops. Suddenly he unleashes, again and again, the words that embody his theme:

"I have a dream that one day this nation will rise up . . ."

"I have a dream that one day on the red hills of Georgia . . ."

"I have a dream that one day even the state of Mississippi . . ."

"I have a dream that my four little children will one day live in a nation . . ."

There are four more "dream" lines. This "dream" sequence—repetition aimed at the gut—is an effective rhetorical device that can serve to mesmerize almost any audience. But more importantly, it builds momentum just when the speech needs it.

Moments later, as he drives to a passionate finish, he tops the whole thing off with another emotional flourish that amps up the intensity even more:

"Let freedom ring from the snowcapped Rockies of Colorado!"

"Let freedom ring from . . ."

"Let freedom ring from . . ."

"Let freedom ring from . . ."

"Let freedom ring from . . ."

Then: "When we allow freedom to ring, when we let it ring from every village and every hamlet . . ." and then a moment later the final words that still resonate today:

"Free at last! Free at last! Thank God Almighty, we are free at last!"

The momentum carries all the way to the final crescendo.

My point is that Martin Luther King Jr. understood that you've got to *build excitement*. He knew that an essentially "flat" speech—with the same energy level in the beginning, middle, and end—runs the risk of sagging, usually toward the finale.

—— THE DANGER ZONE ——

The danger zone typically occurs as we approach the 18-minute wall (Chapter 14), often because most people fail to sustain their energy and momentum. They begin to falter two-thirds to three-quarters of the way through their speeches.

> When you think *danger zone*, think *boredom*, which is to be avoided at all costs. Boredom is the offense for which you will not quickly be forgiven.

Even within the limits of the 18-minute wall, the danger zone is a very real threat. It can unravel any presentation but is most damaging in the prepared text speech. And it can happen for any number of different reasons, sometimes in combination:

◆ The presentation itself is badly designed—with a lot of flab evident in the standard sinkhole that usually shows up somewhere in the last one-third.

◆ The presenter gets bored (particularly if the material itself is boring or the presenter is giving someone else's presentation)—and the lack of interest shows.

◆ Most people who are not professional or experienced speakers will by nature begin to flag after the halfway mark.

◆ Nervousness cripples the entire presentation.

> *The lesson is simple:* If you have something worth saying, let your conviction and enthusiasm show. If you let your convictions and enthusiasm show, the danger zone will go away and the problem will fix itself. The danger zone goes away when your message carries the day—that is, know what you are talking about, translate what you know into a message people can understand, and then let that message build in power and intensity.

Don't worry whether you are too impassioned or too little impassioned. That's not important—leave acting to actors. What's important is first having a message, then believing in it, and then giving that message to the audience in a way that leaves no doubt about your total involvement, commitment, and absolute sincerity. Do that, and the danger zone will quickly become a safety zone.

——— EVEN JUST AN UPDATE CAN ——— BE A CAREER OPPORTUNITY

But not everybody finds that easy to do. CFOs and their staffs, for example, often object when I encourage them to seek a theme or a message, even in a quarterly review. The *review* is the message, they tell me.

Yes and no. Yes, because a review is obviously a review. But no, because an update of any kind is also an opportunity to position the report in a larger, more relevant framework that requires the perspective of leadership. For example, what are the market trends driving the quarter? What changes have emerged that might alter the business? What worldwide long-term developments are in play that will affect the numbers, and why? And above all, where are we going? What is going to happen? What should we do?

So I tell the number crunchers: *add value to what you do.* Start by projecting the future, which is what the listeners are *really* interested in. Articulate the business as you see it in the months ahead; *then* explain that projection based on your conclusions and proposals drawing from the previous quarter. This is what we defined in an earlier chapter as "reversing the wave." In effect, start with the ending. Begin at the top of the wave; then *surf down* the back of the wave toward your ending. That's the opposite of how most presentations are set up. If you were to put it on a graph, it might look like this:

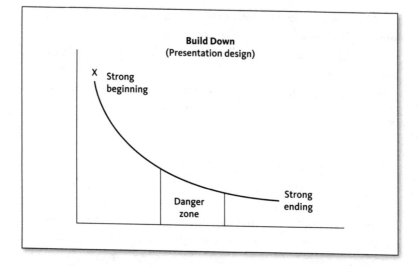

Now consider what we've been talking about in this chapter—the danger zone. To get rid of the danger zone, we've got to *build up*. We've got to get the ball going and then kick it *uphill*. In other words, energy goes *up*.

The next figure shows where you can expect to find the danger zone and how your energy and enthusiasm should carry you *upward* through your presentation.

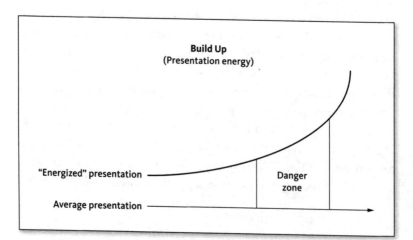

Now it's plain to see that although presentation *design* operates on the principle of a *reverse* wave, the *energy principle* operates on the principle of a *standard* wave. This may seem like a paradox, but together they combine to create a powerful piece of work, which looks like this:

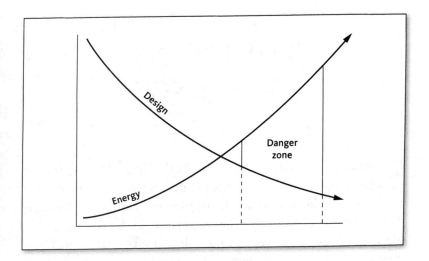

Now you can forget all this and remember only that the great presentation not only has a strong start and finish in its design, but a strong ending also in its energy. To blow away the danger zone, simply:

1. Be prepared.
2. Apply the POWER formula.
3. Care a lot about what you are saying and not so much about how you are doing—and make sure you do not flag in the final portion of your presentation.

22

THE POWER
OF SILENCE

SILENCE IS AN asset, rather than a liability. Most beginning
speakers view complete silence of any kind as an anathema. But
every good speaker knows how to use silence to his or her advantage.
A wise person once said that there is, in any good speech, a greater
message in the pauses than in the words that surround them. There
may be some truth to that. For one thing, most speakers tend to talk
too fast. One reason they speak too fast is because they are always
rushing to fill the dreaded "dead air," these moments of sweat-in-
ducing silence when not a sound is occurring in a room filled with
people. Another reason is that they want it over with as quickly as
possible.

A friend of mine who runs a small business has a recurring
nightmare in which he is standing in front of an audience of blank
faces, unable to make words come out of his mouth. Nothing, not a
sound—only silence. He wakes up in terror, his heart pounding, and
finds it hard to go back to sleep.

This is a person who like so many others is terrified of public
speaking. A famous poll found that the majority of people surveyed
said their number one fear is not dying, but public speaking. Death
was second or third on the list. So we still have a pretty big problem

here, a problem big enough in some cases to affect our work, our sense of self-worth, and sometimes even our careers.

But silence and pauses—the biggest perceived demons in public speaking—need never be our enemies. In fact, they can be our very good friends. Actors understand the value of silence better than the rest of us; they know that pauses can make the difference between a mediocre performance and a great one. What separates the players from the amateurs, so to speak, is what I call the perception-of-time gap. More on that shortly.

The strongest start of all is silence.

First, going back to strong starts, the best way to begin strongly is to begin with nothing. That is, look around the room at your audience, look into their eyes, let the seconds tick by until they are convinced you are going to tip over and have a stroke. Stand in utter silence for four, five, or six seconds, and your silence will fill the room and focus the attention of all the people on you. Where others might begin to prattle nervously, you just stand and say nothing. The sense of anticipation builds through a seeming eternity of passing seconds until at last you say something. And what you say, as you saw in the POWER formula, will further grab their attention. You will begin strongly. You will deliver something of value to them right off the bat.

So silence should occur even before you speak. All the above should happen within our guideline eight seconds.

—— THE PERCEPTION-OF-TIME GAP ——

When I videotape clients speaking, often they cannot believe that the pauses that felt like ages actually appear comfortable, conversational, and normal on the video replay. There is a large gap between the perception and the reality, which we will call perception-of-time gap, a faceless, elusive enemy that we have to tame into submission— or it will rise up to threaten us every time.

I remember having a motorcycle accident some years ago. The time I was actually in the air seemed like eight to ten seconds, yet the real time could not have been more than a second. In a sense, public speaking for some people is a little like a controlled motorcycle accident. The higher the anxiety, the more time seems to stretch.

In moments of crisis, time can appear to almost stand still. Actually, the mind is trying to give the body time to save its own life. Some people call this altered state a heightened sense of "flight or fight." In extreme cases, there may even be enough time to see your life pass before your eyes.

> Understanding that the perception-of-time gap lurks within is essential in mastering the art of public speaking and coming across as a leader.

Don't let discomfort with silence dictate your performance. Fight back the need to race on. Cool it. Slow down. Learn to love those weird and wonderful pauses. If you say something important, for example, just stop. Count to three. Look at the people. You'll be surprised how well pauses actually work:

We have got to take action now. Pause.

Each of us is essential to the success of this company. Pause.

We will never surrender! Pause.

> Control time and you can control your audience.

23

BODY LANGUAGE

I RECENTLY WATCHED A senior businessperson extol the virtues of his company to a large audience. Every time he said "me" or "us," he seemed to slap his chest. Twice he struck the lectern with his fist to make a point, but his timing was off and his points fell embarrassingly flat. Once or twice he said "you" speaking to the audience and suddenly thrust his hands out like an evangelist saving souls. On top of that, he read his speech with his eyes down most of the time.

It was clear to me that someone had tried to coach this man to speak and botched the job. The exec wound up looking self-conscious, rigid, and robotic, with the result that in spite of all the apparent training he did not go over well with his audience.

When you don't go over, neither does your message.

The key to looking and sounding natural—in other words, conversational—is to try to *behave* naturally. People have to move in a way that is true to *themselves*. That's why it can sometimes be more harmful than helpful to try to tell someone to behave, act, or move in a given way for a particular situation. When trainers try to coach clients to respond in a programmed way, the result can be mortifying.

To understand body language, first be aware that no set of guidelines is necessarily right for you. The only real answer to how you should behave is within yourself—and you will find it if you look for it. When leaders speak, they look animated and relaxed. They seem to respond naturally to whatever they are saying. So can you.

So the first rule of body language is that there are *no rules* (short of not acting silly or unnatural, or creating glaring distractions).

The second rule of body language is try to *answer your own heart* when you speak. If you are speaking from a prepared text, for example, try to say the words on the page as if they really were your own and were coming right out of your head (more on prepared text in the next chapter). That's exactly what every good deliverer of prepared text needs—a confident conversational style with a thinking person's text and reactions that come from the heart. Even if you can summon no emotion at all, still try to hear the words in your head before you actually say them. That way, you are far less likely to sound like you are reading.

If you are speaking extemporaneously or from simple notes, it is a lot easier to practice a natural approach, because you don't have to read the speech. Now you can express every idea any number of different ways, with one way not necessarily any better than another. You can be free to warm to your subject and really be yourself.

Even if your options are limited and you find yourself stuck at a podium, you can always count on this short list of easy tips that will make any delivery better:

♦ *Don't sway.* Keep your feet fairly close together. Swaying only makes you look distracted, uncomfortable, in a hurry to finish, and altogether unprofessional. With your feet together, if you reflexively start to sway, you will start to tip over.

♦ *Turn your feet slightly as you move to face different parts of your audience*—sort of pivoting or rotating on the same spot. The trick is to rotate gracefully, without bobs or jerks.

♦ *Keep your head in the same place*, which will happen automatically if you don't sway and if you rotate slowly on the same spot under your feet. (If you choose to leave your script behind and walk around, stand up straight, and of course don't worry about keeping your head in the same place.)

♦ *Use your hands to help animate your talk.* I tell my clients that if hand movements do not come naturally, use short chops of their hands for emphasis and grander, larger gestures (if they feel comfortable with that) to make important points. You can also hold a pen in your hand to give your hands something to do other than folding them across your groin or falling completely limp to your sides. Touch your hands together, open them up—keep them moving. You might let one hand slip into your pocket while using the other to help you make a point, and then switch the free hand into the other pocket and bring the other hand out.

If any of these suggestions seem awkward or uncomfortable, then seek your own counsel and trust your own instincts to tell you what to do and when. President Barack Obama, former president Bill Clinton, and Secretary of State Hillary Clinton, all practice the hand movements we've been talking about with comfort and skill.

If you can get away from the lectern, do so. Now you've got the whole stage. Just be sure to move slowly and never turn your back on your audience. Stop from time to time to make a point or discuss an issue. Don't be afraid to pause for emphasis.

For example, you can ask a question, such as, "What do you think it will take to turn this thing around?" Or make a big statement such as, "This is the most important moment in the history of our industry," and then walk a few steps in silence, stop, and continue. You will see professional speakers using effective pauses like these all the time.

The best way to learn the game is to *practice*. Use the camcorder, use the mirror. Try to develop a conversational style that feels comfortable. Then apply what you've learned in this book and see for yourself how a little practice can go a long way.

24

HOW TO DRESS

L IKE IT OR not, first impressions often count for a lot—so people could get the wrong idea of what you're all about just by looking at you. That's why it only makes sense to dress in a way that creates a minimum of distraction from your message and at the same time enhances how you want the audience to consider you.

> The quick answer to dressing up for the occasion is to wear better-quality clothes that are both simple and basically conservative.

Clearly, this would be the wrong advice for a clown or comedy act or for an informal party atmosphere. But if you're talking about speaking to civic, government, church, or business groups, you can't go wrong by toning down your apparel.

I don't pretend to be a style arbiter or fashionista of any kind, but I do think I can give you some idea of what works and what doesn't.

—— WHAT MEN SHOULD WEAR ——

In general, men would be safe wearing:

- *Better-quality business suits*, dark blues or shades of gray.
- *White dress shirts,* preferably without the button-down collar (a plain collar is more elegant). White is a universal fashion standard and offends almost no one. It's even OK to wear on TV—though for years white shirts tended to "flare" and "ghost" on TV screens. Today the technology is so advanced that white is all right. White also defines good skin color contrast—especially in those wan winter months when many of us who happen to be Caucasian tend to lose that healthy outdoor glow. An alternative is pale blue, with or without pinstripes.
- *Dark knee-length sheer socks* in blue or black (you don't want those pasty, hairy calves poking out at the audience while you're waiting on a panel for your turn to speak; nor do you want those calves showing when you cross your legs in a TV interview).
- *Black shoes only, please*, for blue, pinstripe, or dark gray suits. Brown shoes go better with brown suits, lighter grays, and pastels. And while you're at it, make sure your shoes are well shined and appropriate. In most occasions, lace-up business shoes are better than loafers, for example. Scuffed, obviously cheap shoes may give some people an excuse to form an early, and perhaps unfair, opinion that you might not be able to shake—no matter what you say or how well you think you speak.
- *Conservative tie*—small polka dots, solid color, or regiment stripe. Styles come and go, but these old standbys seem to go on forever. They look smart and keep distractions to a minimum. For years, consultants like myself have been advising client to wear bright red ties, a bolt of color, which draws the audience's attention right to the face and spotlights the speaker. You can see our political clients almost every day on TV fol-

lowing our advice. But you can also see these people, sometimes three in a row, wearing white shirts, red ties, and dark
suits all at a table facing the camera in a "Today Show" interview, for example—and you almost expect one to cover his
eyes, another his ears, and the other his mouth. So the "power
dressing" combo of yesteryear (red tie, white shirt, dark suit)
may not be the ticket for the twenty-first century.

Keep in mind that the suit jacket comes off and the sleeves get
rolled up when you want to give a nonverbal message of informal-
ity—down on the factory floor, for example. Presidents Barack
Obama, Bill Clinton, and George W. Bush always knew when to
ditch the jacket.

The bottom line is that common sense will dictate what is appropriate. Polyester and pastels are probably best left out of any haber-
dashery equation (if you look like a lawyer or banker you might be
forgiven, but a leisure suit, particularly in a business setting, can be
seen as a crime against all reasonable definitions of good taste).

We should note here that good-sized portions of the U.S. Midwest view pinstripe suits and the like with special disdain, so a relax-
ation of the previously suggested guidelines might be in order
depending on the particular location in which you find yourself
speaking. It might even be a good idea to ask the opinion of someone
who is going to be in your audience and let his or her suggestions
guide you. (I remember being told by more than one person in the
Midwest that I looked exactly like what I was—an Eastern Ivy
League city slicker. I needn't add that this sort of thing does not sit
well with a great many people west of the Hudson River. The fact
that I did not necessarily sound like a city slicker—particularly a
New York city slicker—held little sway with these good people, and
I'm sure they put me down as someone capable of a good bit of
white-collar crime.)

In the South and the Southwest, where the weather is warmer,
fabrics get lighter. The darker colors of the Northeast power corri-
dor (Washington–New York–Boston) tend to fade the farther west

and south you go, until the transformation is complete in places like Texas, New Mexico, and Arizona, where the suits seem to blend right into the desert landscape.

Another area in which the rules, such as they are, may change is academia—which is notorious for rumpled geniuses and beret-capped professors in ancient tweeds, long scarves, and baggy corduroy pants. Still, when I speak to business school audiences, I stick to my standard bankers-issue dress code, and that seems to be all right. The students or executive program people expect someone who looks like a business consultant, and that's pretty much what they get—but you won't find a lot of professors who dress for the job the way I do.

We should also mention that in recent years Hollywood has brought us pony tails and baggy Italian drape suits, sneakers, shades, jeans, T-shirts and tuxedo jackets for formal evening wear, and a lot of artsy black ensembles for day or night. Comfortable stuff, no doubt, and some of it not bad looking, either. But you've got to be an acknowledged eccentric, the best in the world at what you do, a pioneer or visionary like Steve Jobs (who favors turtlenecks, jeans, and sneaks in public appearances), or independently wealthy to be able to imitate Jack Nicholson or Don Johnson in front of a business audience. Leave the black silk shirt and high tops in the closet.

However, hundreds of companies have taken to designating Fridays as a day of casual dress code, so the times they are a-changing. But if you are scheduled for a business meeting with a client on a "casual" day, you should still wear a suit and tie unless specifically requested not to.

There are whole sections of California, most notably Silicon Valley, where any pretense at conventional business dress went out the window years ago. If you go to Silicon Valley on business, it's best to call ahead and ask what your client thinks is appropriate—particularly if you plan to make a speech or give a presentation. However, San Franciscans—especially those in financial services—tend to dress like New Yorkers.

____ WHAT WOMEN ____
SHOULD WEAR

Women who speak a lot either in business or in politics seem to prefer conservative business suits. Barring that, they will generally opt for dresses that look expensive yet give no suggestion that the wearer is trying in any way to appear sexy. Of course, naturally presentable women cannot help that they do, in fact, sometimes look attractive to men in their audiences—but no woman speaker in her right mind, even in our politically correct times, should lose any sleep over that simple truth or consciously try to change it. Common sense demands, for example, that the neckline not distract.

Women speakers' business suits tend to span a wider color spectrum than those of their male counterparts. Pastel colors, for example, are not uncommon. Bold reds and blues are the most popular of the bright colors.

Hemlines go up and down, but the best-dressed and most experienced women speakers seem to be telling us:

1. Keep it simple—stick to conservative suits and dresses in solid colors.
2. Reduce jewelry to a minimum, thereby cutting down on distractions from the face and eyes.
3. Go easy on eye makeup.
4. Don't wear hats when you speak—unless you are outside, or happen to be a member of the British royal family.
5. Use scarves whenever appropriate to add a certain flair and style of your own without appearing to be too fashion-conscious.

Over the years, many of my corporate clients have been women who have on occasion expressed personal concerns about speaking in public. Some have confided to me, for example, their discomfort about having to follow a particularly robust, commanding male speaker. They know, correctly, that their voices are not as deep or resonant and perhaps do not carry as well. The contrast, they are afraid, will not only diminish what they have to say but also heighten the potential that the audience may take away an incorrect perception that the woman speaker lacks leadership, strength, or other qualities. These concerns are all understandable and legitimate. But they are also manageable.

First, it is true that any speaker, male or female, who seizes and practices the simple protocols in this book, can fare better than all but the most dynamic speakers—sometimes even without formal training. That's the first point.

The second point is that the soft voice, if used correctly, can be as imposing as the deepest of baritones. That's why we've got microphones. I encourage my female clients to make certain in advance that the microphones work well wherever they have to speak. Some of the better mikes do not have to be any closer than two feet to pick up and amplify even the gentlest voice. If my female clients have to speak without a mike, I ask them to get as physically close as possible to their audiences and then bring their voices up "short of a shout"— that is, speak loudly enough so that they can still look and sound natural and at the same time be heard by even the people in the back rows. A number of experienced women politicians know how to do this very well. Naturally, if you go beyond "short of a shout," you will, in fact, be shouting, and that is not desirable.

Volume and projection, then, are fixable. But a slightly tougher problem is presented by the client whose voice falls into a soprano register—what one woman client ruefully calls her "Mickey Mouse" voice. The truth is she does not sound like a Disney character, but her voice is by nature more highly pitched than the average female voice and stands out sharply in every business meeting and every presentation.

In the end, I referred her to a voice coach, who changed my client's breathing and rate of word delivery and helped her come down a notch or two on the falsetto register. This added depth and also beefed up her volume, so that today she feels a lot more self-assurance when she's called on to speak.

Asking clients to boost their volume "short of a shout" is about as far as I am willing to go on the subject of projection. Someone without any real speaking history, stage experience, or theater training can only sound inadequate or unnatural when trying to project his or her voice with too much gusto. So if you find yourself in a big room with a lot of people and no microphone, don't overdo it. Remember:

Say it with clout just short of a shout.

25

HOW TO READ A
PREPARED TEXT
LIKE A PRO

(and Not Look Like You're Reading)

PREPARED TEXT DOES not make sense for everyone. For most people, speaking from notes or an outline or even extemporaneously is more effective and certainly more believable. But sometimes prepared text is the clear choice. For example, when:

The legal beagles insist you say every word on the page.
There is a consistent party line that everyone in your organization has to adhere to.
You have a precise time slot to fill.
You have no preparation time, and the speech is prepared for you by someone else, or you find yourself having to give someone else's speech.
Your speech has an accompanying slide show requiring rehearsal and precise cues.
You feel more confident and comfortable reading from a text than trying to speak extemporaneously or from notes or an outline.

Reading from a script while trying to appear not to be reading is a neat trick. But that is exactly what we may have to do if we are burdened with a text and expect people to take us seriously and listen to what we have to say. Few people—either in public or private life—know how to handle a prepared text properly. Unless they are using teleprompters, even U.S. presidents look like they are reading a text verbatim.

No one can master the art of prepared text delivery from a book—because until now *no book* has been able to explain correctly how it should be done. But a few simple tips, plus some practice in front of a mirror, can still make a measurable difference in how you come across.

—— DON'T SHOOT 'TIL YOU SEE ——
THE WHITES OF THEIR EYES

The key to great prepared text delivery is disarmingly simple. Most people, when they speak from a script, begin almost every sentence with their faces and eyes pointed down at the page. They come up for air in the middle of the sentence and then dive right back down to catch the words at the end of the sentence. Repeat this action three or four hundred times and you've got a pretty dull presentation. Graphically, this looks like:

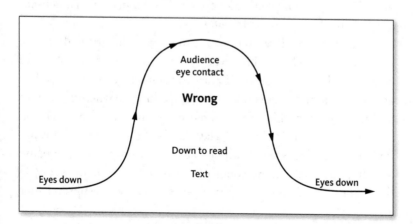

Even if the words are great, the speech will fail in the presentation.

The answer is to reverse the procedure. Instead of starting each sentence with your eyes on the text, begin each sentence actually looking straight at the audience. Then allow your eye to scan down to read the middle of the sentence right off the page. Then bring your eyes back up to end each sentence looking back at the audience again. Repeat that several hundred times, and you will not look like you are reading the speech. The correct way looks like this:

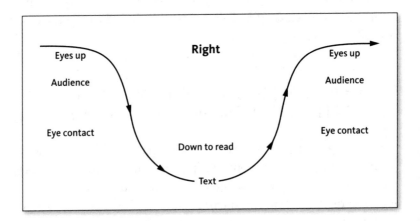

If you like, choose a few faces in the audience all the way from your left to your right and spend a few seconds with each face, one at a time, every time you make eye contact. So instead of *down-up-down,* you are now doing *up-down-up.*

The trick is to allow your eyes to memorize the first half or so of the sentence in silence. Then you bring your eyes up, establish eye contact, and speak the words. Before you run out of words, you allow your eyes to return again to the sentence, picking up where you left off and reading the middle of the sentence right off the page. Then you raise your eyes again to finish the last part of the sentence. All this you do in one seamless sweep with no pauses. The only times you pause are after you establish eye contact (for just a beat, to make sure you don't "cheat" by speaking before your eyes are all the way up) and after each sentence (for emphasis and to make sure you don't dive down for the next sentence before you're finished speaking).

Imagine you are on a stage looking at an audience. If you are playing the game correctly, you are looking directly at your listeners as you speak to them. You are now in what I call the GO ZONE. If you are looking over their heads, somewhere up in the ether (maybe because you are not a practiced player and find all eye contact a little disconcerting), you are in what I call the OZONE. If you are looking down, or below the level of eye contact, you are in the NO ZONE.

Look them right in the eye, and you are in the GO ZONE. The longer you stay in the GO ZONE, the better your presentation will be.

The place to be, obviously, is in the GO ZONE. Stay out of the OZONE entirely and visit the NO ZONE only when you *have to* (for example, to grab a line of text). That's why, if you *must* use a prepared text, you must also know how to deliver it so you remain in the GO ZONE most of the time and don't look like you are reading.

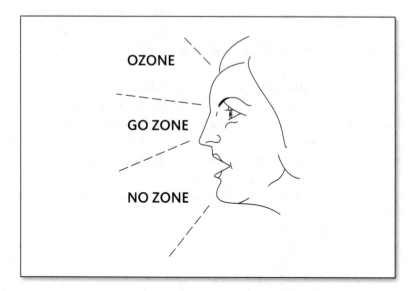

But even if you understand the *up-down-up* idea, chances are that you may still wind up speaking too fast because your mouth will be tempted to try to catch up with your eyes. So *always leash yourself in.*

Put on the brakes. Consciously slow down, and you will probably end up sounding conversational.

And remember to *pause often.* Pause after every sentence. Stop after every key point. Saturate your audience with eye contact. Really look *at* the people and not over their heads.

—— TEXT ——

The up-down-up drill sounds easy, but for people not used to it, it can feel awkward. To make the procedure as easy as possible, prepare your scripted speeches so that:

1. *The letters are big enough to be read easily from three to four feet away.* Laser printers can quickly produce enlarged conventional typeface, which should be one-third- to one-half-inch high.
2. *Each sentence is a separate paragraph.* (This makes it a lot easier to execute the drill we just discussed.) If the original text has several sentences in a paragraph, you can indicate which separated sentences belong to the original paragraph by not indenting those sentences. They would still be separate, just not indented on the speech copy. The only indented sentence would be the lead sentence of the original paragraph.
3. *Double-space each sentence, and triple-space between each paragraph.*

4. *The last sentence on the page should end on the page.* The sentence should never continue to the top of the next page (again, easier to track with your eye).

5. *Put page numbers in **all four corners**.* (Life being what it is, you want to avoid having to genuflect for five minutes if you should drop your speech on the way up to the podium.)

You will now have more pages, but you can easily move each page with almost no distraction. While looking at the audience, just slide the page over as you speak the words from the last sentence on that page.

When you are ready to go, your pages should look something like this:

We are who we are, and that's

as it should be.

But most of us live our whole lives

not having a clue about who we might

have been.

One way to find out who we might

be is to venture outside our own

expectations . . . to make new

footsteps.

That's what good speakers do . . .

they surprise themselves, and then

they begin to find themselves.

Prepared Text Basics

◆ Use large laser print easy to read from at least three to four feet away.

◆ Use *upper*case and *lower*case.

◆ *Separate each line* with a double space and each paragraph with a triple space.

◆ Make *every sentence* a separate paragraph.

◆ Put page numbers in *all four* comers.

—— POSITION ——

Position yourself slightly *away* from the lectern. You don't have to go to MIT to figure out that the angle of attack for your eyes is less steep the farther back you go. This lets you keep your chin and face up while your eyes go down to the page and do all the work. Your eyes, remember, track down to the page *only in the middle* of sentences. Short sentences are simple: you just take them in their entirety.

Just by standing back a few inches you automatically increase your eye contact. You should be twelve to eighteen inches away from the lectern, far enough to let you express yourself with your hands if you wish to, yet close enough to still touch the lectern (many people like the comfort of feeling "grounded" to something solid).

Some lecterns are adjustable. If you know in advance you are going to use a prepared text, you should make it a point to request an adjustable lectern. This is particularly important for tall people. Adjust the lectern so that the top of the front is just below your sternum (and just below where your heart is).

—— HANDS ——

Short of creating a distraction, try to let your hands help you express yourself, for two reasons:

1. Freeing up your hands to "talk" with you helps vent the anxieties that you may feel about speaking in the first place. People experience anxiety or stage fright in different ways. But when allowed to build without release, anxiety can reveal our fear by making us look nervous or wooden. Nervousness often manifests itself in rocking or swaying. Using your hands helps hide fear by physically releasing tension. Keeping your hands active can also help compensate for the frustration of feeling stuck at a lectern.

Of course, your hands should not run away with you. They should always help, never distract. So keep your moves disciplined: short chops to make points, fingertips touching, palms up, palms down, a fist in the palm, all done with some discretion and restraint. Or, as we mentioned in the last chapter, you could keep your hands busy by holding a pen and occasionally switching the pen from one hand to the other.

2. In addition to releasing tension, your hands can also help make you look a lot more natural. You feel more spontaneous and sound more conversational. Curiously, your voice seems to gain confidence and you may even find yourself on a roll. But it's hard to be on a roll if your hands never move from your sides.

Some further points:

◆ If you insist on keeping your hands folded behind your back, you may wind up looking a little too much like a bad imitation of Prince Charles.
◆ Arms folded across your chest is a nonverbal signal that you feel vulnerable. You look like you're protecting yourself and would probably rather be someplace else.
◆ Hands raised up to your sternum (heart) with fingers touching is almost priestly.

—— FEET ——

By contrast, as we mentioned earlier, if you have to stand at a lectern (and if you have a prepared text, you most certainly do), then you also have to position yourself in one place and stay there. Paradoxically, I tell people that rather than stand planted with their feet apart, they ought to place their feet fairly close together, six inches or so.

The reason for this is simple. Most people with a prepared text become anxious or bored and start shifting their weight back and forth from one foot to another. This is enormously distracting and sends the signal that you're not really committed to, or even involved in, what you're saying. By contrast, as we have said, if you put your feet close together and try to shift your weight, you'll probably tip over. Plus, you'll gain another inch or two in altitude, and sometimes every little bit helps.

But now that you are stuck in one spot, you'll feel trapped unless you have some way to move around a little. The answer is to stay in the exact same place, but to *turn slightly by small moves of your feet* to face different parts of the audience (some of the best political and evangelical speakers do this well).

So let your hands keep moving (perhaps occasionally touching the lectern—never gripping or tapping the lectern) and let your feet keep moving, too. If you move your feet gracefully, the audience will hardly notice that you are moving at all.

—— SHALL WE DANCE? ——

Now let's quickly walk through what happens when you're called up to speak. Listen carefully to the introduction. The person doing the introducing might say something very personal, poignant, or even witty. Sometimes these seemingly offhand remarks just beg for a response—and if you don't respond, you could appear to be not plugged in to what is happening around you. With luck, you will be able to respond with a line that not only spins off the introduction but also makes a business point relative to what you've come to talk about.

But don't push your luck. If you have a prepared text and can't figure out a way to weave in a one-liner without hurting your strong start, forget it. Just go ahead and begin the way you had planned.

If you are carrying your speech with you (i.e., if it is not already waiting at the lectern), conceal it as much as possible by wrapping it around your thigh away from the audience. So as you walk to the lectern, you are carrying the speech close to your leg.

You have already *memorized at least the opening line* or two, perhaps the first couple of sentences, so there is *no* need to look down once you get to the lectern. When at the lectern, still trying to keep your manuscript hidden, ease the speech onto the lectern. Look at your audience while you're doing this. If you are right-handed, place the body of the speech on the left side, with the top page on the right. Reverse that procedure if you are left-handed. With the speech spread out this way, you won't have to move the page for at least the first minute or so.

Now position yourself back far enough so you can still touch the lectern, but at the same time have a good angle for your eye to hit the page. If the lectern is adjustable and someone else spoke before you, adjust the lectern so the rear portion is just below your sternum.

Once you begin speaking, slide the pages over as needed—*never turn them.* Sliding will minimize the perception that you have a prepared text and help give the impression you are speaking from notes or an outline. This, in turn, will reinforce the perception that you are not reading—which can only mean that you know what you are talking about. After five or ten minutes you might begin to get a little antsy—but *resist* the temptation to let it show by rocking or swaying (see Chapter 23).

Here are some additional tips:

Stay vigilant and alert to what you're saying. Borrow from the actor: actors *hear their words in their heads* before those words come out of their mouths. So use your pauses as you glance down at each new sentence to *listen to the words* in that moment of silence before you actually say them. Do this hundreds of times, and the effect will be that these words are, in fact, your own—even if someone else wrote them for you, or you are giving someone else's speech.

Pause *longer* after rhetorical questions and key points. Those pauses may seem agonizingly lengthy (remember, the adrenaline has probably been working overtime), but to the audience you will only look natural, thoughtful, conversational, and comfortable with your subject.

When you finish, *don't bolt*. Stay long enough to keep your eye contact with the audience. If there is applause, simply say "Thank you," pause for another moment, and then leave the podium.

Remember *never* to show the audience your entire prepared text—if you can avoid it. Slip the speech discreetly off the lectern and leave it on the shelf underneath, or slide it back to whichever leg is out of sight of the audience as you walk back to your seat.

Prepared Text Basics
- Eyes *up-down-up*, not *down-up-down*.
- *Don't "shoot"* 'til you see the whites of their eyes.
- Pause *before* speaking and *after* speaking.
- Use *longer pauses* after "credibility" lines and questions.
- Let your *hands* help you do the talking.
- Keep your *feet fairly close together* so you don't sway.
- *Turn your body* to face different parts of the audience.
- Position yourself *away* from the lectern for better angle of eye attack on the page.
- *Slide* pages, don't flip them.

I should add this important note of caution: learning to give a prepared-text speech as if you were just speaking extemporaneously requires lots of practice. As a rule, I spend only two or three sessions on this skill with corporate people. But with politicians, the work sessions can number five or six—because their jobs depend on being able to use one prepared text after another and *never* appear to be reading (often in outdoor venues that do not favor the use of tele-prompters, but where a prepared text is deemed essential).

In a later chapter I will talk about self-training. But the rule for using prepared text is simple:

If you practice at home in front of a mirror and can't see your eyes, you're doing something wrong.

The most common arena for prepared text is the big presentation, the big (or important) audience, and the big PowerPoint that goes with it. In fact, most prepared-text speeches involve visual aids of one kind or another.

Now that you know the rules for prepared text, I would still advise that you resort to a verbatim script only if you absolutely have to.

26

HOW TO USE
TELEPROMPTERS

I F YOU LOOK closely, you will often see politicians and officials on TV or in real life standing behind lecterns flanked by what appear to be little glass shields, which are sometimes mistaken for special bulletproof security devices. But these glass plates are actually tele-prompters (also known as autocues), which help speakers give speeches without having to look down at a script.

Teleprompters are one-way mirrors, which are supposed to be almost invisible to the audience but provide a large-type scrolling text visible only to the person behind the lectern. Their functional beauty lies in the fact that they put the speaker perpetually in the GO ZONE.

Obviously, teleprompters do not make sense in smaller rooms with smaller audiences because they are much easier to detect. In fact, they can quickly become a distraction at the expense of the speaker. Up close, it doesn't take long even for people who have never seen one before to figure out what they are. On top of that, with the lectern bracketed with "shields," it can look like you have insulated yourself from your listeners behind a kind of barricade. With busi-ness and political audiences alike, this does not go down well. So a business leader using a lectern and teleprompters in a boardroom, say, would *only be shooting himself or herself in the foot.* Trying to use one in an outdoor venue may be impractical. But in a large venue on an indoor stage removed from the audience, they can be very effective—provided you know what you are doing.

Of course, it would always be best if you could appear before any audience *without* a teleprompter—and still look like you are speaking without a text. But to do that, you would have to become skilled at prepared text delivery, which we talked about in the last chapter. That might take some time and self-training (or a crash course with a coach like myself). So if you cannot or will not use a written text, you are not talking to a smaller audience, and you cannot manage the "presentation" extemporaneously or with simple notes or outline, then teleprompters are your best bet.

Here are some rules for using teleprompters:

If at all possible, try to make sure you or a trusted associate who can be your eyes and ears has a chance to meet in advance with the teleprompter operator. You want to be certain the equipment is working well, that the script is loaded properly (and with the correct script), and that the operator is experienced enough to scroll the "crawl" to your individual delivery—fast, slow, or dead stop, right with you every syllable of the way. If you have a chance to rehearse, even better. A good operator will be able to *anticipate, adapt,* and *adjust* to your style.

Check the font. Is the type big enough? Can you read it at a glance? The font should not be too big nor too small. Both screens will carry the same crawl simultaneously.

Uppercase and lowercase font is easier to read than all caps. Choose black text on a white screen or white text on a black screen.

Now you should be ready to go. But if you have had little or no experience, you might wind up bouncing back and forth from one screen to the other like a spectator watching a fast tennis match at the U.S. Open. This "Ping-Pong" effect is a dead giveaway that you are a novice. To perform like a pro, follow these tips:

Instead of just reading the words, try to capture maybe an entire *half sentence*, or perhaps a whole short sentence. Before you speak, try to get a sense of the meaning of those words. If the text is yours, this should not be a problem. Now, with these words in your head you are free to let your eyes *move away* from the screen—either to the left of the left screen or to the right of the right screen. This now puts you *outside* the predictable play area and gives the impression not only that you are not wed to the screen, but that you are making an effort to reach the outer edges of your audience. Veteran teleprompter users do this routinely.

Let's say you begin with the left screen. When you have delivered your words (to the left of the left screen), you can now let your eyes return to capture the rest of the sentence and continue speaking as your face now moves across *the audience directly in front of you*. This transition leads you now to the right screen, where you can pick up the last words of the sentence and *continue beyond the screen*.

Then your eyes slip back a couple of degrees to the right screen again, where the scroll has presented you with your next sentence. You now seize the first half of the new sentence and reverse the process, this time working your way from right to left. This way, you are not playing Ping-Pong. You are moving smoothly and speaking to *all* the audience, left, center, right, and beyond. You are starting to look like a pro. With a little practice, your delivery can appear effortless.

Do not rush. We read faster than we talk, so take your time. Pros never rush. Remember to breathe normally. Take a big breath between sentences, because any pause is a good thing. And a breath between every sentence automatically gives you opportunities to create lots of pauses.

You may have noticed that this technique requires a kind of horizontal version of the up-down-up protocol that you read about in the last chapter. If you don't happen to have a teleprompter at your disposal, and you don't have a professional coach, practicing up-down-up in front of a mirror at home will help prepare you for the teleprompter.

In the unlikely event that the equipment fails, always have a text copy (properly formatted—see previous chapter) with you at the lectern. You may want to put a green or red dot in the scrolling "crawl" text to signal you when to slide your hard copy page over—just in case the crawl suddenly disappears. At that point, you had better have some familiarity with the prepared text delivery skills we talked about earlier, because to go straight from the teleprompter and the GO ZONE to reading a text verbatim on the lectern in the NO ZONE can look like the rhetorical version of a train wreck.

27

TAKING A CUE FROM
STAGE MONITORS

I F YOU FIND yourself on a stage and want to have the freedom to move around (which I would encourage), you will find stage monitors useful.

Stage monitors are essentially flat-screen TVs, usually discreetly hidden near the edge of the stage from audience view, that make it possible for you to give your whole talk without prepared text, teleprompters, or even physical notes or outline. You can use them as your own private high-tech cue cards, or they can reflect the entire presentation, slides and all, in which case, what you are looking at on the little flat screen at the foot of the stage is also visible simultaneously to your audience on the big screen behind you.

The trick with stage monitors is to try not to let on that you are using any kind of support system at all. In other words, try not to let the audience catch you spending a lot of time looking at the edge of the stage, talking to the floorboards.

The *only* way you can pull this off and come across as an outstanding speaker is to master the up-down-up technique for prepared text we discussed in Chapter 25 and in the previous chapter on teleprompters. Your objective is to have *100 percent eye contact* with your audience, while roaming the stage at will. To do that, you must *not* speak while checking your cue on the stage monitor. Speak *only* when you are back in eye contact with your audience.

Those pauses may feel awkward to a beginner or anyone new to the game, but experienced speakers appreciate them—and so do audiences.

You may look like you are glancing down for a moment to think about what you want to say next—this is *exactly* the impression you want to create.

You may elect to have several monitors tucked away along the stage perimeter—one on the left, one in the middle front, and one on the right. Or you may just want to have two in the front, one on the left and one on the right. As you move around the stage (careful not to move too quickly or to turn your back on the audience), you now have wide access to your monitors and absolute freedom not available to any speakers, save those remarkable few who need no cues, props, or visual aids of any kind.

Before you actually use stage monitors, you should hone your prepared text up-down-up skills and get comfortable with the newness of working with cues below eye level.

PART FOUR

AFTER THE SPEECH AND MANAGING THE MEDIA

28

THE ART OF Q&A

IDEALLY, YOU SHOULD be as facile and engaging in your prepared text delivery as you are in your question-and-answer (Q&A) period afterward. But it's more likely that you will feel more comfortable and judge yourself more competent in Q&A. Since Q&A may in fact be your strongest suit, it only makes sense to strengthen whatever aptitude you already bring to the party. Here are some guidelines you should keep in mind.

Be alert—don't relax after the formal speech. Businesspeople are *constantly* confronted with questions. Some of those questions can be hostile, depending on sensitive or controversial issues in the workplace, prevalence of sexual harassment, equal opportunity, women and minority representation, animal testing, toxic waste, air and water pollution, or white-collar crime, for example. So don't get caught off guard. *Be prepared—even for the worst.* And remember that the Q&A encounter is actually an opportunity to *redeem* the situation if you feel things have not gone particularly well during the formal presentation.

If you are concerned about getting the ball rolling, station a "plant" in the audience to ask the first question.

Turn any Q&A session to your favor with your own agenda. This means that regardless of what you may be asked, come prepared to make several points. You may wish to reinforce what you've already said in your presentation or to add something that you forgot or didn't have time for, or to hammer home an overriding message. To direct the Q&A session the way you want it to go, use what the media people call "bridging." This simply means answering any question the way you want to answer it. For example:

> *"Consumer activist groups are complaining that your company is not passing the savings from the recent drop in oil prices along to consumers at the gas pumps. How do you answer that charge?"*
>
> REPLY: *"I think the real question is, how do you measure real savings after we have spent a year keeping our pump prices artificially low in the face of skyrocketing oil costs?*
>
> *"When everyone else was high, we were low. Now the market is fluctuating up and down, but our prices are still relatively low.*
>
> *"And keep in mind that one out of every three dollars we take in goes to oil exploration. That's an investment in our future that will make us self-sufficient—and the only way I know of to guarantee low prices at the gas pump."*

This person is obviously prepared. She bridged by saying, "I think the real question is . . . ," which immediately seized control of the conversation and put the ball in her court. Then she jumped straight to three points she wanted to make.

Caution: Bridging, if done consistently, is sometimes viewed as evasive. So bridge sparingly and wisely, saving the bridge only for the hardest questions.

The following are examples of some other bridges:

"That's much too involved an issue to try to answer in the short time we have here, but what I would like to say is . . ."

"I don't think anyone can give a realistic answer to that question, but what I can say is . . ."

"We've heard that question before, and we'll hear it again, but what we're not hearing is . . ."

"I don't know the answer to that, but what I do know is . . ."

More bridges:

"The more important question is . . ."

"Sure, that's important. But have you thought about . . . ?"

"Instead of that, you should ask me about . . ."

I remember the example of the Dow Chemical executive who was asked on national TV about the devastating role of Dow's napalm product in the Vietnam War. The executive replied that while war was tragic, Dow had just developed a vaccine for meningitis in children.

Sometimes you can deflect a pointed question by invoking legal or corporate protocol:

"I'd like to answer your question, but our lawyers have asked me not to just yet, because the matter is still in litigation. What I can say is . . ."

"We'll have to withhold our answer until we've had a chance to review all the facts."

"We have decided to hold off until senior management has had a chance to look at the facts and agree on an appropriate response."

"We can't talk about that until we know more—because if we do, we're afraid someone might get hurt."

Bridging assumes you have something to bridge to, so arm yourself with a list of points; then take the time to rehearse your answers to tough questions with an associate.

Don't answer too quickly—for three reasons. A pause before answering first gives you time to think your answer through before talking. This will likely shorten your response, get rid of those talking-while-thinking "uhs" that are only a way to buy time while you think, and eliminate redundancies. Second, a pause tells the audience that you are a thoughtful person who doesn't shoot from the hip. Last and most important, it provides a consistent pause in the event you're asked the patently unfair or unexpected question that comes right out of left field. *With a consistent pause before all your answers,* you won't appear to be reeling when the tough question finally does come. And the people asking questions won't spend the remaining time dwelling on that issue.

Tell the truth. Whatever you do, don't lie—because you'll probably get caught. If you don't know an answer, say so and then offer to provide the answer as soon as possible. Or if the truth hurts, then be prepared in advance to deal with that issue.

Be concise. Try not to overanswer. We're all guilty of talking too much at some time or another. But talking too much in Q&A can be *counterproductive.* For one thing, most listeners are comfortable with conversational "sound bites" of roughly eighteen seconds, and if you talk longer you should have good reason. (If you don't think eighteen seconds is a long time, check your watch and count off eighteen seconds of silence. It's actually a surprisingly long time.)

If you have thought about questions and answers in advance, there should be little reason to give long answers. Besides, long, rambling answers often signal a poor preparation, fuzzy thinking, discomfort, and redundancy.

Get right to the point. This is a point I can't stress enough. A person thinking clearly won't build to an elegant conclusion. Rather, the Q&A master will often jump right to the main point (reversing the wave) and then explain briefly how he or she came to that conclusion.

A good example or two will go a long way to providing credence.

If you do have good examples, don't be shy about busting right through the eighteen-second "sound bite" to go longer than eighteen seconds.

Stay cool. Don't get into a spitting match with a skunk because you're bound to lose. Stand your ground and be firm if someone is taking shots at you, but also try to be courteous.

Be sincere. Simple sincerity is a winning grace. Humor can be a useful weapon in a hostile interview, but try to avoid coming across as a comedian. Often humor is seen as sarcasm or insensitivity and can backfire.

Beware of false premises. You may get a question that is based on incorrect facts. If so, correct the facts and set the record straight before you go on to answer that question. However, if the questioner uses egregious adjectives such as "howling," "unwise," "stupid," or "incompetent," ignore the provocation and forge ahead with an answer, perhaps a bridge, that lays bare the lie and turns the situation around.

Don't say, "No comment." We hear "no comment" all the time on TV, but these two little words provide a lot more problems than solutions. "No comment" suggests that you are stonewalling—even though you may not be.

I remember the story of the oil company CEO who cautioned his vice president of corporate affairs never to speak to the press without first consulting with the CEO. One day when the CEO was away on a fishing vacation, a tank farm blew up, throwing flames hundreds of feet in the air. When the newspeople showed up, the hapless vice president stood in front of the fire saying "No comment" over and over. Of course, he had nothing to hide, but the next day local headlines hinted darkly of a secret nuclear facility or special government top secret weapons program gone bad.

To avoid this unnecessary embarrassment and still satisfy his CEO, the vice president need only have said something sensible like, "We have a problem and we're working to fix it. As soon as we know more we'll let you know."

When several questions are asked by the same person at the same time, don't feel obliged to answer more than one. Pick the one you like, answer it, and then move on. If you wish to answer all the questions, you may have to take a couple of notes, or ask the questioner to repeat the remaining questions.

During the course of the Q&A session, *don't respond to the same question twice*—even if it is worded differently. Say that you have already answered that question and move on.

If, in the beginning, you have no "plant" and no one seems to want to ask the first question, ask yourself a question to get things going.

Don't prolong the Q&A period. When you are past the prescribed time limit or sense the meeting has gone on long enough, say something like, "We have time for one more question," answer that question, and then stop.

Record the session. It's helpful to have a video or audio verbatim transcript—not only so you can see how you did, but also if the subject matter is particularly sensitive. It's not a bad idea to have your own record of what you actually said.

29

DEALING WITH
THE MEDIA

A RECENT SURVEY REVEALED that *more than half* of all executives polled so distrust TV reporters that they would flatly refuse to be interviewed on television under any circumstances. This is understandable, given the aggressive "ambush" nature of "Sixty Minutes" and its subsequent imitators over the years and considering the generally antibusiness bias behind most TV stories involving corporations.

Yet for those who feel they have a story to tell and are willing to view the medium as a stepping-stone rather than an obstacle, television is an opportunity *almost too good to pass up*.

Handled properly, one free minute on network TV can be worth more than a year's fees to Madison Avenue.

Here are a few suggestions:

Consider yourself on the air from the moment you walk into the studio. No need to be paranoid, but keep in mind that careless chatter with an associate about what you should not be saying could be overheard by an ambitious production assistant and wind up on the air as an unwelcome interview question.

Care more about the message and the points you want to make than how you are doing. If you do this, you probably won't have to worry about how you are doing, because your commitment and focus will gather momentum and carry the day.

Know your show. What is the show's format? Controversy? Confrontation? Political? Social? Bizarre? Is the host bright, stupid, angry, ambitious, liberal, or conservative? Does he or she prepare thoroughly? Or does the host reveal more style than substance? Knowledge of what you are getting into can give you a better idea of how to conduct yourself.

Think the right thing. Rather than picture yourself in a defensive posture, take the opposite view and go on the offensive.

See yourself, as Sarah Palin does—love her or loathe her—as someone on a mission, a prophet of enlightenment.

Try to be positive, helpful, and enthusiastic. Clarify and instruct. Give vivid examples. Take a genuine interest in trying to convey your answer or point of view in the most helpful way you can.

Don't attack your opponent. That's just bad form—especially when he is not there to defend himself. Feel free to question logic, reasoning, or conclusions, but resist the temptation to impugn one's character or motives. People who stoop to personal attacks can themselves be seen as suspect.

Avoid "secret handshake" language that smacks of the corporate, bureaucratic, or heavily academic. It's a "home," not a "domestic habitation unit." It's a "death," not a "hospital care negative outcome." It's a "bond," not a "fixed-income vehicle." It's a "doctor," not a "primary health care deliverer."

Listen carefully. How well you do can depend on how well you listen. If you are on a panel show or a show with a central point of origin and other people at several "remotes," pay attention to all the questions and all the answers. Be on the alert for "loaded" questions based on false, misleading, or openly hostile premises.

Be yourself. Need we say more? Don't try to change or act out a role, because you may wind up looking and feeling fake.

If pressed hard, question the questioner. Years ago in a memorably contentious campaign interview in the 1980s, George Bush (senior) suddenly counterattacked and started asking pointed questions of Dan Rather on national TV. The tactic clearly caught Rather off balance and left Bush looking like the victor.

Plan your quotable quotes in advance. In an interview there's nothing like a clever label or phrase to grab people's imaginations. Churchill coined "iron curtain" and "summit conference." Other familiar standbys are "silent majority," "new deal," and "cold war." You may not see yourself as another Churchill, but you can use evocative standbys such as "ticking time bomb" or "accident waiting to happen" to reinforce your case.

Use statistics sparingly and wisely. Reinforcing your point with statistics adds credibility but can clutter your message. Stick to no more than two statistics per point, and—as always—*keep it simple*. For example, "83 percent of people polled said they support the measure, but only 15 percent said they would be willing to pay extra taxes." Or you could simply say, "Eight out of ten Americans say they support the measure."

Cite your personal experience. Whenever possible, draw on your own eyewitness recollections. There is no substitute for actually having been there. For example: "People complain about bureaucracy and how they never seem to get anything done. But in the three years I spent in local government, I saw more projects completed than in the previous twenty years spent in a big corporation."

Defuse loaded questions. Techniques for doing this include: (a) disagreeing with the loaded premise ("I don't agree with your characterization of American managers"), (b) recognizing that some people may agree with the loaded premise ("It may be true that some people feel the way you do, but . . ."), or (c) bridging immediately to your position ("It may be true that some people feel the way you do, but most people fail to consider that . . .").

Don't be afraid to change your mind. It's OK to change your mind. More than one major reversal in a lifetime is probably too often, but we should feel free to change our minds about issues as the circumstances surrounding those issues change. Robert McNamara, the former secretary of defense under Presidents John F. Kennedy and Lyndon Johnson, and chief architect of America's aggressive military involvement in Vietnam, changed his mind. Years later, McNamara finally admitted he had been wrong in Vietnam and wrote a book about it. A change of heart can signal flexibility and open-mindedness, so admit when you've changed your mind and be prepared to explain why.

Assume the microphones are always "hot"—even before and after the show, or during commercials. This means don't say anything you wouldn't be comfortable saying on the air or having immortalized on tape. No one wants to become part of a "blooper" reel.

Try *not* to nod when interviewers are asking you questions. You know that your nod is a courteous sign that says, in effect, "Yes, go on, I understand," or "I am listening." But on TV your nod, particularly in conjunction with a hostile or pejorative question, can seem to mean, "I agree with your damning assumptions," or "Yes, I am guilty and ashamed." Feel free to nod *only* if you happen to be in wholehearted agreement.

Wipe sweat off your brow with your finger, not your handkerchief. TV lights can sometimes be uncomfortably hot, and it is not uncommon for people to perspire. If you feel beads of sweat developing, try to discreetly run your forefinger along your brow. Should you choose a handkerchief, it would look like it was the question, not the lights, that is making you sweat. Using your finger can actually give the impression that you are thoughtful.

Never play to the camera's little red light. Instead, keep your eyes on the host or other panelists at all times, and try to imagine that you are having a conversation that approximates a relaxed social situation. The studio director controls the action, so don't waste your time trying to find the "on" camera. You will only wind up looking distracted and untrustworthy. Besides, unless you are a professional on-air "talent,'" you will appear to be grandstanding.

Never look at yourself in the monitor. In most studios, the monitor will be hidden from view, but if it is not, resist the temptation to check yourself out and see how you look. You will appear distracted and inane to people watching. Instead, concentrate on the host or panelists and later request a tape of the show.

Try to be as "likable" as possible. Likability counts for a lot on TV. You can measure likability in several ways: by staying cool and reasonable under a bullying attack, by showing a sense of humor, and by being prepared with facts and figures and revealing a genuine desire to enlighten and be helpful. It is conceivable that you could feel you fared badly during the interview, yet wind up actually getting high marks—based on nothing more than how well you came across.

Try to be crisp. The average on-air news "clip" of people talking is only eighteen seconds. That's perhaps eighty words or less. Because of the demands of available airtime and deadlines, tape editors will typically favor the shorter cut for later broadcast. **Best solution:** If you feel you can answer the question without bridging, go straight for the conclusion, with a fact, figure, or anecdote to back it up. You may even have some time left over.

30

HANDLING HECKLERS

THERE IS NO easy way to defuse hecklers, but you need never be the victim of someone who tries to steal your platform and grandstand at your expense.

Humor can be a *potent weapon* in the right hands. Former Secretary of State Alexander Haig was once speaking at the United Nations when a group of Puerto Rican separatists began shouting at him from the first row of the mezzanine-level spectator's gallery. Without missing a beat, Haig stopped his speech just long enough to say that he was unable to hear what the men were trying to say, but "if you would just step forward a few feet I'm sure I could hear you a lot better." The audience laughed, and the hecklers sat down and stopped heckling.

In a political campaign, any heckling can be an opportunity for the heckled. In a famous campaign coup that has since been imitated and repeated by many other candidates, President Ronald Reagan responded to loud heckling by saying, "This, ladies and gentlemen, is why I'm here—this is democracy in action. The very system that these people are complaining about is the system that makes it possible for them to be here shouting at the president of the United States. And I, for one, intend to protect their rights as long as I'm in office."

Fictional personal attacks are fairly common. Take, for example, the heckler who shouts something like, "When was the last time you cheated on your taxes?" This largely rhetorical question is intended to draw attention to the questioner at the expense of the person being heckled. It is meant to cast, by suggestion, a bad light on the morals or character of the speaker, while endowing the heckler with the higher moral ground. But more often the tactic backfires, and the heckler winds up looking like the bad guy.

You might recast that loaded question this way: "The question has come up as to whether I pay my taxes like everybody else. The answer, of course, is yes. Next question?" Or you might want to put a light touch on the situation by taking a stab at humor: "I admit the thought has actually crossed my mind. But my wife tells me I'm a bad liar, so I think I'll leave cheating to those who have a much higher tolerance to gambling and the risks of living dangerously."

The chances of your being heckled in most business or civic speaking situations are not high. But it's always nice to be prepared. The key objectives when dealing with hecklers are:

- ◆ Be firm.
- ◆ Be courteous.
- ◆ Control the situation.

Sometimes it's tough to be courteous and hold your ground at the same time. But hecklers have no intention of engaging in rational discourse. Hecklers throw caution to the winds. They bully and grab all they can when they can, leaving most of their targets feeling frustrated and violated and without a clue of how to appropriately respond.

Here are a few simple tips that could help if the going gets tough and someone starts heckling:

Deflect the heckler. Listen for five or six seconds, long enough to appear courteous and until you can be certain you're dealing with a real heckler who does not intend to shut up. *Counterattack by firmly interrupting the diatribe in progress.* Butt back in by assertively asking the question, "Are you asking me a question, or are you making a statement?"

If the heckler responds that he or she is asking a question, then demand the question. Now the control of the conversation rests again with you. The heckler asks a question, and you can respond by (1) dismissing the question with a simple "yes," "no," "of course," "perhaps," or "maybe" and then quickly moving on to the next question; (2) bridging to a point you want to make; or (3) answering the question honestly and sincerely, without elaboration. The idea is to *dispose of the question as quickly as possible* and to press ahead in another direction.

If the heckler responds that she or he is making a point, you quickly cut in to remind the heckler that the time available will not allow statements—only questions—but that you or a representative would be happy to meet the heckler afterward to discuss the issue further. Then, of course, you should show good faith and make good on that pledge.

If the heckler won't back off and won't stop the disruptive behavior in spite of all your best efforts, then you have no choice but to turn to another part of the audience and ask for another question. Remember, in most cases, you have the microphone. If you don't have a microphone, forge ahead anyway. If there is no other question forthcoming, you can always ask *yourself* a question, such as: "People frequently ask me, 'What is the toughest part of your job?' And my answer often surprises them. My answer is . . ."

If the heckling continues, you can caution the heckler that if he or she does not sit down and let other people be heard, then you won't even agree to meet afterward. Or you can threaten to have the heckler taken out by security. Or, as a last-ditch defense, you can declare the Q&A session at an end, thank the audience, and leave.

(Don't forget to turn off the mike when you go.) This last tactic could be viewed as a victory for the heckler, so it should probably be used *only in extreme situations* when things are clearly getting out of hand and there seems to be no chance of regaining the floor with dignity. Typically, you would have to be facing more than one very enthusiastic heckler to be forced to take this action.

Rephrase the question. Sometimes a heckler, when pressed to ask a question, will counter with some heavily biased vitriol so loaded with innuendo that it just begs to be recast as a simple declarative sentence. Not only does rewording the question remove the sting, but recasting makes the question a lot easier to answer.

For example, an angry former employer shows up at a new product launch and shouts: "Why don't you tell them about the pollution your factory is pumping into the town's groundwater every day?"

Your response could be: "The question is . . . what are we doing to improve the environment in our community? The answer is . . . a lot . . . and there's nothing secret about it." (Then explain your pollution initiatives.)

Happily, heckling is infrequent. The first heckle is always the toughest. If you expect to be a leader in your business or organization, you can expect a little heckling from time to time. You can also expect to surprise the heckler.

31

TRAIN YOURSELF

PEOPLE WHO TEACH golf, skiing, and tennis have known for years that nothing speeds the learning process like showing someone a tape of themselves trying to perform a test of skills. The subjects of these revealing videos study every move and every nuance with uncommon attentiveness, because they are, after all, watching themselves—and they don't always like what they see.

The same is true for the role of the TV camera in helping people (1) see themselves as others see them, (2) spot distracting body movements or gestures, (3) practice for speaking assignments, (4) perfect key elements like pauses and eye contact, and (5) monitor their own progress and improvement as they advance through a program like mine to develop their own speaking styles.

Even if you have never had even a single minute of professional help or speaker training of any kind, regular use of a camcorder setup with a tripod and TV monitor in your own home or in your office will help make you a more effective talker. The reason is that most people are acutely sensitive to whatever shortcomings may show up on tape. Once you identify the offending elements, *it is easy enough to practice until they go away.* It is important, though, that you don't see a swan as an ugly duckling and then proceed to kill the swan. So I suggest that if you undertake to practice with a camcorder, you also undertake to apply the principles you learn in this book. If you don't have a camcorder, can't afford one, don't want one, or can't rent or borrow one, you can practice with a mirror. Practice the POWER formula. Practice the 8-second drill. Practice prepared text. Experiment with eye contact and pauses for emphasis.

You may also wish to identify with your favorite speakers in government, business, or show business. If you think it can help, borrow whatever attributes you see in them to perfect your own speaking game.

However, if you don't trust yourself to get it right (because you're not sure what you're supposed to be looking for—even after reading this book) and if you are really serious, you can always hire someone to help you. For individuals this could be seen as an extravagance. But for a corporate person or someone running for public office, private training is an abundantly rewarding investment that makes good business sense. (Of course, one could argue that paradoxically, people like me are part of the problem. We may have done our jobs too well—because some of our clients in politics and in business have only added to our fiscal and regulatory woes.)

The golden rule, which I mentioned earlier, bears repeating:

If you can't see your eyes—that is, if your eyes are not eye level the whole time you are talking—you're doing something wrong.

Advanced technology, mass production, lowering cost, and the demands of the information age have made it possible for more people than ever before to have access to affordable, high-quality camcorders (handheld television cameras with built-in recorders and playback capability). For people who want to become good on their feet, no tool is more useful or more informative.

32

WHAT'S IT ALL WORTH TO YOU?

ALL OF US, like it or not, will eventually see our reputations, careers, and even our social lives determined to some degree by how well we speak. Are we forgettable—or do people remember us and act on what we say? Are we boring—or do we spark interest and get people involved? Do we hide our intelligence and potential by the way we speak—or reveal ourselves in the best possible light? *Our own words will likely shape our lot in life.*

The degree of our success will be determined by our powers of articulation, our vocabulary, and our mastery of the English language.

People will judge us—fairly or unfairly—on how we present ourselves face-to-face in countless moments of human interaction. The phenomenon I am talking about is what I call *leadership communications* (leaders lead with their words), issues management (what to say, when, and to whom), time management (let's not spend more time than we have to preparing), productivity (are they getting the message?), effectiveness (did we get results—did they do what we wanted them to do?), and profitability (can we attribute our growth, profit, and good fortune to how we position ourselves and tell our story?).

Even how we answer the phone can have an effect on our future. An inarticulate response in a meeting can torpedo an important deal or sabotage a whole career. Poor eye contact and mumbling can put an end to hopes of advancement in any organization.

Is it possible to put a dollar amount on the business value of good leadership communications skills? I remember when the new CEO of a company said to me, "You know, this stuff is great, but I don't know how to measure it. I don't feel like I can get my arms around it." The CEO came from the finance side of the business, so he tended to feel uncomfortable without specific yardsticks to mark progress. He was challenging me to reassure him that the money he was spending on speaker training was a good business investment.

My answer was simple. I told him I did not know, either, how to render an exact measurement. But I reminded him of the first time we had worked together, shortly after he had become CEO. My assignment was to prepare him for his first series of analysts' meetings. We met three times in two-hour sessions. The day after the first analysts' meeting, the stock shot up forty-five points, producing a paper profit to the corporation of a little less than $100 million.

So I told him that by any reasonable measurement, if he credited the work we did together for just one-tenth of 1 percent of that share price increase, my fee was still just incremental by comparison. He could only laugh.

Each of us has it within ourselves to shape our own destiny—and it's an exciting prospect to know not only that there is always room to grow, but that it's actually fun to constantly improve at whatever we do. When I was a boy, I learned to ski. I still ski. When I was a bit older, I learned to ride a motorcycle. I don't drive a motorcycle anymore, but I could if I had to. The same goes for playing tennis, playing golf, and flying a plane.

Once you learn the rules and the moves, you can play the game. The more you play the game, the better you get. The better you get, the more fun you have. The more fun you have, the more likely you are to be successful at whatever you do.

But as I said in the beginning, we have given ourselves over to the wonders of media technology. We have been utterly *seduced* by our BlackBerry phones (I am a Crackberry addict myself), e-mailing, texting, Tweeting, blogging, surfing YouTube, plus interacting with hundreds of new and ingenious handheld apps—all the sexy magic of social media and beyond—often at the expense of our own professional and corporate futures. In a sense, we have thrown in our lot with all the dazzling toys at our disposal.

But I think we may be betting on the wrong horse. The fortunate few who see this rapid cultural change as an opportunity, and recognize that the articulate executive is becoming ever more rare, can break out of the social media loop and position themselves as leaders—while their peers and competitors are lost in the daily distractions of technological innovation. In other words, they can make of themselves prized commodities.

Bottom line: Social media aptitude and BlackBerry expertise will never take the place of two people taking face-to-face or one person talking to a thousand. Interacting live, in real time one-on-one, eyeball-to-eyeball, and pressing the flesh will trump text messaging and e-mails every time.

This is how the product gets sold and the deal gets done. This is why the investor reaches for the checkbook, the troops outperform the competition, the customer asks for more, the order is won, contracts are awarded, relationships are sustained, and partnerships cemented.

Yet in the United States today, very few people ever learn to play the speaking game. If they do play, they often play by the wrong rules—as we've seen in these chapters. I see a lot of lost opportunity for millions of people struggling to make it in a tough, often unforgiving business universe. How much easier their jobs would be, I am convinced, if they would but learn to play the game.

Becoming a player can be surprisingly easy. Simply understanding the basics in this book and then applying them can make a measurable difference *right away*.

If you are just beginning, it might not hurt to join a platform organization like Toastmasters International. This is a nonthreatening environment in which you can practice. *The more practice the better.* You can get a feel for the game, have fun, and afford to make a few mistakes. Once you learn to command the room and influence audiences, you are on your way. *One success breeds another.* Soon you will discover the thrill of the game and understand, perhaps for the first time, how incredibly powerful words can be in business and life itself.

The payoff can be so rewarding, there should be no excuse for not making a conscious decision to alter our own lives for the better:

> for the CEO who wants to be seen as a leader
> for the COO who wants to be CEO
> for the CFO who wants to drive the stock straight up
> for the lawyer who wants to serve her clients better and build her practice
> for the salesman who wants to run his own region
> for the researcher who wants to help his clients and his own management understand the incomprehensible
> for the team leader who wants to see better performance in his unit

for the teacher who longs to inspire her students
for the entrepreneur who seeks investors to build her business
for the leader who wants to be a transformative leader
for the transformative leader who wants to be a threshold
   leader
and for all the toilers in all the vineyards who ever wanted to
   leave the world a little better than the way they found it

The payoff I am talking about will work for anyone willing to work for it. *Mediocrity is not inevitable.* The way out of mediocrity is implementation—simply using what you read in this book.

So don't waste a minute. Start playing the game tomorrow. Seize the opportunity, and see for yourself how far you can go.

TEST YOUR NEW ARTICULATE EXECUTIVE IQ

—— ARE YOU A PLAYER? ——

Now you've read the rules and positioned yourself for rapid advancement. But are you ready to play? To call yourself a master of leadership communications, you've got to internalize what it takes to outperform. If you really want to excel, it's well worth reviewing the fundamentals. To get started, ask yourself a few quick questions:

What constitutes a perfect presentation and the POWER formula? *(Chapter 7)*

How can I begin strongly and end strongly? *(Chapters 8 and 12)*

How can I use the rocket? The necklace? *(Chapter 13)*

How can I capitalize on the 18-minute wall and the 8-second drill? *(Chapters 14 and 15)*

How can I reverse the wave? *(Chapter 15)*

What constitutes the basics? How does the Oreo work? *(Chapter 16)*

What is the difference between the Whopper and the Wafer? *(Chapter 17)*

How can my team really look like a team? *(Chapter 17)*

What are the most common language mistakes? *(Chapter 19)*
Why is *up-down-up* so important? *(Chapter 25)*
Why is the GO ZONE so important? *(Chapter 25)*

Answers to these questions are the kind of game-changing knowledge you'll want to have in your pocket every day of your working life.

Here's a checklist you might find useful:

- Forget opening amenities. If you must use them, throw them in only after a strong start.
- Remember the POWER formula: *P* (punch/strong start), *O* (one theme), *W* (windows/examples), *E* (ear/ordinary language), *R* (retention/strong ending).
- Begin every presentation without slides (unless it's a blue or black blank slide, title, logo, video, or montage).
- End every presentation without slides (or return to logo or blank slide).
- Skip word slides in the actual presentation itself, but save them for the handout or official document (hard copy or digital).
- Instead of word slides, use only charts, tables, schematics, and photos.
- If you must use word slides, use only brief quotes, lists of products or people; instead of bullets use just one word or phrase, such as a large centerpiece banner in the middle of each slide. Limit banner words to one slide each.
- Stick your slides in the middle of your presentation.
- Avoid white backgrounds, and go easy on the pastel colors.
- Make slides simple (make them complex only when complexity is the point you want to make).
- Use just one image per slide (unless you're preparing a presentation deck).
- Use presentation decks that are thin (Wafers). The handout documents can be as fat as you want them to be (Whoppers).

Execution

- Roll in to the next slide while the old slide is still up (an eight-second introduction to the business point of the next slide).
- Click to the next slide only after you've finished the roll-in.
- Operate in the GO ZONE audience eye level. OZONE is too high. NO ZONE is too low.
- Don't hand out hard copy ahead of time—(unless the client or customer insists).
- Distribute hard copy only after the presentation.
- In team presentations, take care of the housekeeping, such as introductions, before you sit down at the table.
- In sit-down presentations, use silent clues (no introductions) to achieve seamless transitions from one presenter to the next.
- If you use a lectern, step back far enough (maybe two or three inches) so you can keep your head up. Let your eyes do all the work (checking your text, notes, or outline).
- If you use a prepared text, use uppercase and lowercase, enlarge the words, double space, make every sentence a separate paragraph, don't track sentences to the top of the next page (finish your last sentence on the same page), and put numbers in all four corners.
- Remember, it's UP-down-UP with your eyes, not down-UP-down.
- Breathe a lot—especially between sentences.
- Practice pausing for effect.
- When you're finished, try asking, "What do you think?"

Rules

- Live by the 8-second rule: Audiences will decide within eight seconds if you're worth listening to.
- Respect the 18-minute wall: Audiences will tune out if you go beyond this psychological barrier. (If you must go longer, include another speaker, show a videotape, tell relevant anecdotes, and throw in more Q&A.)

◆ If you can't define your theme in eight seconds, either you don't have a message or you don't know it.

Dress
◆ Keep it simple. Keep it conservative. Invest in quality.

Stage Fright
◆ If you think less about yourself and how you're doing and more about your message and how it's going to help the people you're talking to, you may never have to worry again about how you're doing.

Other Tips
◆ Be prepared.
◆ Think of your audience as family and friends.
◆ Imagine those times you thought you did well.
◆ Remember that it always feels worse than it looks.

This is the moment when the rubber hits the road—because now you can begin putting your new competitive knowledge to work to start reaping your hard-earned rewards.

For example, do you have an important event coming up? Begin right now to plan for your next:

◆ Keynote address
◆ Quarterly review
◆ Industry speaking engagement
◆ Management report
◆ Sales meeting
◆ TV appearance
◆ Strategy meeting
◆ Board meeting
◆ Media campaign
◆ Panel discussion
◆ Convention seminar
◆ Annual meeting
◆ Analysts' meeting

- Fundraising effort
- Marketing or sales campaign
- Team conference
- Investors meeting
- Awards dinner
- Job interview
- Employee assembly

These are all rich opportunities for competitive advantage, advancement, profit, and growth—as long as we know how to unleash our new knowledge and skills to make things happen and get measurable results with all these different audiences.

For instance, let's say you have a speech to an important industry audience coming up next month. Last year the same assignment might easily have become an ordeal and source of anxiety. But not today. Because today you've got POWER and the BASICS working for you. You've got the rocket and the necklace and you understand the 18-minute wall, among other things.

The first question you've got to ask yourself is: What is my theme, what is my message?

So what *is* your theme?

Don't know? Take a look around at what's going on in your business and in the economy and then think about what you see. Still not sure? Sit down with associates or partners. If you set out to find your voice, or your theme, you will find it.

Try to come up with an interesting viewpoint or original approach to an old problem—or any angle that might allow you to claim a leadership position.

Still can't find it? Then try the 8-second drill. Pick a subject that you think is the sort of thing you might want to talk about it. Give yourself three minutes; then work your way down to eight seconds (see Chapter 15). The eight seconds you wind up with are by definition your theme. The 8-second drill automatically produces your message because those eight seconds are a pure distillation of everything you started with.

For convenience, and to keep it all in one place, I now invite you to try to articulate a theme that can become, in a sense, your "party line," your "marquee message," the issue or objective that matters most to you (or your company). This is your opportunity to create a "voice" for you or your company that you may never have had before, a theme you can apply to a wide range of speaking opportunities.

Journalists call this an "evergreen" story because it never changes as long as it remains useful.

Take some time to think about it; then write it down—maybe just a sentence or two—right here in this book:

_____

_____

_____

_____

_____

_____

Once you've got your theme, you're on your way. Everything else falls in place. Now the second question you should be asking yourself is: How should I start, and how should I end? Keeping your theme in mind, take a quick look at Chapter 8. Then write down three ways you might want to start strongly (you can use just one, all three, or more if you like):

1. _____

_____

_____

_____

_____

2. _____

_____

_____

_____

_____

3. _____

_____

_____

_____

_____

If you really want to be creative, you can also consider starting with a video or music, or both. Now write down three ways you might want to end strongly:

1. _____

_____

_____

_____

_____

2. _____

_____

_____

_____

_____

3. _____

_____

_____

_____

_____

The third question you should be asking yourself is: How am I going to prove my case? What kind of compelling evidence can I come up with? You should be able to make an ample list. Pick the strongest—perhaps the top five—and write them down here:

1. _____

_____

_____

_____

_____

2. _____

_____

_____

_____

_____

3. _____

_____

_____

_____

_____

4. _____

_____

_____

_____

_____

5. _____

_____

_____

_____

_____

And that's about it. See how surprisingly simple it is? The gnarly business of preparing presentations demystified—forever! No more headaches, no more worry. Preparation time slashed to almost nothing. Effectiveness enhanced almost immeasurably. The only thing left now is to get up, go out, and do it.

As I said at the beginning, nothing in business presents greater opportunities than making your case face-to-face with important audiences. If I were you, I'd think of every audience as important. Social media may he helpful, but it will never take the place of you.

To make sure you understand how much I believe in every word you have read in this book and how much I sincerely want you to succeed, I am offering you my personal e-mail. You may reach me at gtoogood@toogoodassoc.com. I will make every effort to respond promptly and do everything I can to get you up and running. This is a first for me. I have never entered into an interactive relationship with my readers. But if you care enough to reach out, you deserve a response, and I am certainly willing to help.

The starting gun just went off and the game is on.

INDEX

ABOUT THE AUTHOR

G RANVILLE TOOGOOD IS a top leadership communications coach, international speaker, consultant, and writer. Prior to starting his own company in 1982, Mr. Toogood was a television reporter and network news producer for NBC and ABC. Today he works with a long list of blue-chip clients and has served as a consultant to more than half the Fortune 500 CEOs, as well as thousands of business leaders, entrepreneurs, senior-level executives, elected officials, diplomats, and celebrities throughout the world. This book is based on his acclaimed leadership workshops in executive communications. Mr. Toogood lives in Darien, Connecticut.